Somerset Thinking Skills Course

Handbook

Nigel Blagg
Marj Ballinger
Richard Gardner

Basil Blackwell

© Somerset County Council 1988

First published 1988
Published by
Basil Blackwell Limited
108 Cowley Road
Oxford OX4 1JF

British Library Cataloguing in Publication Data

Blagg, Nigel
    Somerset thinking skills course.
    Teacher's handbook
    1. Study techniques – For schools
    I. Title   II. Ballinger, Mary
    III. Gardner, Richard
    371.3'028'12

    ISBN 0–631–90271–6

The authors began work on the Somerset Thinking Skills Course in 1985. The original team consisted of Nigel Blagg, Senior Educational Psychologist, and three teachers: Marj Ballinger; Mel Petty and Gareth Williams.

In 1986 Gareth Williams returned to teaching and Richard Gardner joined the team. Mel Petty returned to teaching in 1987 leaving the remaining members, Nigel Blagg, Marj Ballinger and Richard Gardner, to continue with the developmental work.

Illustrations by Richard Gardner
Typeset in 11/13 pt Palatino
by Photo-Graphics, Honiton, Devon
Printed in Great Britain

Dedication

The Somerset Thinking Skills Course is dedicated to the memory of Barry Taylor, Chief Education Officer of Somerset 1973–87.

Acknowledgements

We are particularly indebted to Barry Taylor, whose charismatic leadership and far-sightedness led to Somerset's involvement with Reuven Feuerstein's ideas and the development of our own cognitive skills course.

We should also like to record our appreciation to Professor Reuven Feuerstein of Hadassah – Wizo – Canada Research Institute, Jerusalem, and Dr Frances Link of Curriculum Associates, Washington, for providing us with the pre-literacy skills to think about thinking and the theoretical frameworks which have formed the basis of much of our work.

We have been enormously helped by many professionals who have broadened our theoretical ideas and directed our attention to important areas of research. In particular, we should like to record our gratitude to Professor John Annette, Warwick University; Dr Bob Burden, Exeter University; and Dr Michael Shayer, King's College, Chelsea, London University.

We have received many useful suggestions for additional activities and modifications to existing ones from teachers in our pilot schools: Blake School, Bridgwater; Castle School, Taunton; Chilton Trinity School, Bridgwater; The Merrifield Unit, Taunton; Monkton Priors School, Taunton; Sydenham School, Bridgwater; Cowes High School, Isle of Wight; Hartcliffe School, Bristol; St Marks School, Bath; Whitecross School, Lydney, Glos. We are very grateful for this help and for their continuing enthusiasm and commitment. We also appreciate the efforts and participation of the many pupils who helped to trial the materials.

During the period of our developmental work, we have been encouraged by advice and positive comments from the many HMI that have visited us. We are especially grateful to Staff Inspector Turberfield and HMIs Wardlow and King who have taken a particular interest in our work.

Finally, we should like to record our thanks to the Advisers and Education Officers who have supported our work. In particular, our thanks go to Janet Bond, Special Needs Adviser; James Clifford, Deputy Chief Education Officer; Don Parkinson, Area Education Officer; Stuart Wilkinson, Education Officer (Special Education), Somerset County Council.

Preface

Somerset Education Authority first became involved in the teaching of thinking skills in the early 1980s. A few schools in the Authority took part in an exploratory trial of Reuven Feuerstein's Instrumental Enrichment (IE) Programme, organised by the Schools' Council. Four other LEAs were involved in the study, and its cautiously optimistic findings were reported in *Making up our minds: An Exploratory Study in Instrumental Enrichment* (Weller and Croft, 1983).

In 1983 Somerset obtained substantial funds from the DES under the auspices of the Lower-Attaining Pupil Programme. Much of this money was allocated to a more extensive trial of IE. Dr Nigel Blagg, Senior Educational Psychologist, was seconded to evaluate the effects of the programme on the pilot pupils, teachers and schools. The final outcomes of this work are still being written up (Blagg, 1988). However, the implications of Feuerstein's ideas and the potential applications to mainstream pupils become apparent at an early stage in the project.

Accordingly, in 1985 Somerset set up a curriculum development group led by Dr Blagg, with the brief of producing its own Thinking Skills Course specifically designed for mainstream children. The curriculum group brought together psychological expertise, teaching experience and artistic skills. The outcome is the Somerset Thinking Skills Course.

Contents

Introduction

The Somerset Thinking Skills Course (STSC) consists of a series of modules designed to teach, discuss and generalise specific concepts, skills and strategies involved in problem solving. Modular themes emphasise different issues, including: gathering and organising information; analysing complex subjects and comparative thinking. The carefully sequenced pupil activities include a variety of tasks to maintain novelty and enhance the possibility of transfer of skills. Each module is intended to provide material for approximately 30 hours of curriculum time.

It is not enough merely to provide a set of materials for classroom use. Simply exposing pupils to different problem-solving activities is unlikely to lead to generalisation of skills to fresh contexts. It is essential to consider the crucial role played by the teacher as a mediator in this process. Accordingly, each pupil activity is accompanied by a set of clear and comprehensive teacher guidelines designed to give easy access to aims and objectives as well as offering a suggested format for each lesson and advice on effective mediation.

This introductory *Handbook* considers a range of theoretical and practical issues related to the Somerset Thinking Skills Course. In particular, it discusses the nature of intelligence and the extent to which intelligence can be taught. The course has been significantly influenced by some of Reuven Feuerstein's theoretical ideas, along with the practical experience and research oucomes of using Feuerstein's *Instrumental Enrichment Programme* in Somerset schools. In view of this, the handbook does provide a brief account of the important features of this work.

Although Feuerstein's work has served as a springboard for the development of STSC we have departed very significantly from his ideas. In particular, the design and structure of the course has been affected by current curriculum trends emphasising active learning methods, and by recent ideas from cognitive psychology about learning to learn. In an attempt to facilitate transfer and generalisation we have drawn upon many different contexts and familiar scenarios in addition to more abstract and unfamiliar problem-solving tasks. Above all, we have taken into account pupil interests and classroom practicalities in mainstream schools. We have aimed to structure and sequence the materials so that they can act as powerful developmental tools, at the same time bearing in mind the need to produce a viable package for classroom use.

The *Handbook* provides a detailed working model which integrates the various theoretical issues underpinning the course. This model includes an analysis of the thinking skills targeted in STSC. The structure and sequence of the various activities within and between each of the modules is reviewed, together with a more detailed consideration of a number of key classroom issues referred to in the Teacher Guidelines for each activity. These include general guidance on the nature of effective mediation as well as specific advice on ways of organising and managing lessons to facilitate group work, class discussions, oracy skills and greater pupil involvement. Particular emphasis is placed upon ways of helping pupils transfer skills learnt in the course to other subject areas, everyday life and the world of work. A further section details ways in which the materials can be used diagnostically. Finally, the handbook considers a number of practical issues including various timetabling arrangements, cross-curricular links and the different ways in which the materials can be used for different age and ability ranges.

1   Intelligence and Learning

The nature of intelligence

For many years it was believed that we each possess a certain amount of a mysterious quality known as 'intelligence'. Although there have been numerous definitions of intelligence, such as 'the ability to profit from experience', the concept has stubbornly resisted clarification. The idea of 'general intelligence' (g) was promoted in the late nineteenth century by Francis Galton, who also believed that the characteristic was inherited. In the early part of the twentieth century, Binet developed the first standardised intelligence test. For much of the time since then psychologists have been preoccupied with assessing intelligence; connotations of its meaning have been closely intertwined with the techniques for measuring it.

In recent years the notion of intelligence being some kind of fixed general capacity has been challenged from numerous quarters. Many research studies have demonstrated that intelligence, as measured by IQ tests, can be radically changed by educational experience (Clarke and Clarke, 1976). At a more fundamental level, however, the whole status of intelligence as a hypothetical construct is undergoing a major reappraisal. One can speculate about the sorts of problem-solving tasks that involve intelligent functioning and then consider the mental processes involved in them. Recent developments in information-processing models of cognition (Sternberg, 1982) have done just this. Detailed analyses of the processes underlying many intellectual tasks have been undertaken and attempts have been made to further analyse these 'components' into clearly defined 'sub-components'. Increasingly, it is being recognised that these sub-components can be taught, leading to the idea that prolonged and systematic teaching can significantly enhance cognitive ability.

Sternberg illustrates these ideas by considering the example of solving an analogy, eg 'Hand is to glove as foot is to . . .?'. As in most problems the subject must first of all decide what processes to use and how they should be sequenced to form a workable strategy. The actual processes selected will involve forming a clear mental image of all the relevant attributes of the elements in the analogy. Next the relationship between the first two terms in the analogy will be inferred from a comparison of their many attributes. Finally, the relationship inferred from the first part of the analogy will·be related to the second part of the analogy. The whole process can thus be reduced to a series of relatively simple comparisons in which related pairs of attributes of 'hand' and 'glove' can be linked to common attributes of 'foot' and some other object – in this instance, sock.

In the context of changing notions about the nature of intelligence and learning, the clinical work of a small, independent team of workers in Israel, led by Professor Reuven Feuerstein, has attracted extraordinary interest. Feuerstein, inspired and influenced by Jean Piaget and Andre Rey, developed his ideas and beliefs in the context of dealing with the assessment and education of orphaned, traumatised immigrants coming to Israel after the Holocaust. Over many years of clinical work, Feuerstein has come to believe in the enormous plasticity and modifiability of the human intellect, and in the crucial role played by significant adults in the child's cognitive development.

Feuerstein emphasises that, while direct exposure to a rich range of stimuli is important, the child's cognitive development is more crucially affected by mediation. In this process features of the environment are emphasised, interpreted, extended and embellished, ensuring that the child builds up an internal model of the world in which disparate aspects of experience are meaningfully related. Thus, the child who is surrounded by many fascinating experiences and opportunities may still be cognitively deprived if there are no significant adults mediating the various stimuli. Furthermore, children with sensory deficits or emotional problems may be unable to receive, or may even block out, both direct and mediated forms of stimulation, leading again to cognitive impairment. Nevertheless, Feuerstein believes that this outcome is not inevitable provided the child receives enough intensive mediation. Feuerstein and his co-workers have been unpacking the nature of mediation so that the adult's role in bringing about cognitive change can be clearly defined. Certain aspects of mediation appear to be culture-specific but Feuerstein claims to have identified and operationalised a number of universal ingredients in the process. We will return to Feuerstein's ideas about mediation at a later stage in the handbook.

Assessing intelligence

> What children can do with the assistance of others might be in some sense even more indicative of their mental development than what they can do alone. . .
>
> (Vygotsky, 1978)

Children learn to learn in a social context. Indeed, for Feuerstein, the parent-child interactions involved in the process of passing on cultural values are at the very basis of cognitive development. Naturally, the child who has been deprived of the opportunity for extensive verbal interactions because of emotional problems, impoverished social conditions or some other reason, will come to any formal traditional IQ test grossly disadvantaged. Furthermore, the standardised instructions and administration procedures provide very little opportunity to explore what the disadvantaged child might be able to learn given more favourable conditions. For these and other reasons, many psychologists have come to believe that traditional IQ tests do not provide meaningful information about the child's potential ability to learn but instead merely indicate what a child has been able to learn to date.

> It is indeed curious that we use intelligence tests mainly to predict capacity for learning and yet none of our tests involves any learning, instead they give us a cross-section of what has been learned.
>
> (Vernon, 1969)

Furthermore these 'static' forms of assessment offer very little in the way of guidance about the kinds of teacher interventions required to bring about cognitive improvements in the child. There is now a growing movement of psychologists in the USA developing and testing dynamic approaches to assessment to complement traditional static forms of intelligence testing. Basically, the dynamic testing procedure involves assessing the child's ability to perform a set of problem-solving tasks in a traditional way without any assistance. This is followed by a training period in which the adult attempts to teach important processes involved in the tasks. The child can then be re-assessed on closely related materials to check for acquisition and retention of the processes that have been taught. The use of progressively dissimilar problem-solving materials involving more complexity (more bits of information); changes in mode (verbal, pictorial, numerical etc); and tasks involving different mental operations, in theory provides the opportunity to assess the flexibility and generalisability of the pupil's newly acquired cognitive skills.

Feuerstein and his colleagues have been particularly active in the dynamic assessment field. Over the past 25 years they have developed a collection of dynamic assessment materials and a comprehensive manual, collectively called *The Learning Potential Assessment Device* (LPAD). Linked to this assessment procedure is a set of curriculum materials known as *Instrumental Enrichment* (IE) intended to offer teachers a set of 'tools' to teach the prerequisites to thinking, thereby making up for a lack of mediation. We will discuss IE in more detail at a later stage.

In attempting to understand the components involved in any mental act and at the same time to appreciate the cognitive demands on the learner, Feuerstein proposes the use of a 'Cognitive map'. This model covers seven dimensions – content, modality, operation, phase, complexity, level of abstraction and level of efficiency. Some of these dimensions are difficult to operationalise, but nevertheless they do provide a useful orientation for the teacher in thinking through why any one particular child is experiencing difficulties with a particular task. The diagnostic value of this framework is examined later in this handbook under *Diagnostic Use of STSC Materials*.

Learning to learn

> It is not your business to teach him the various sciences but to give him a taste for them and methods of learning them when this taste is more mature. This is assuredly a fundamental principle of all good education.
>
> (Rousseau, 1762)

Recent ideas about the nature of intelligence are complementary to recent developments in the 'learning to learn' movement. 'Learning to learn' is not a new idea, but it has rarely been central to curriculum planning. Yet in a rapidly-changing technological world, when it is difficult to predict what knowledge will be essential or useful for the future, developing self-knowledge and the ability to 'learn to learn' is surely more important than ever before.

Concerns about these issues have been reflected by a growing consensus among those who argue that the traditional curriculum has prevented many children from demonstrating and developing their intellectual capabilities. Many educationalists now recognise that even those pupils who have demonstrated success within the traditional system by passing examinations, often find themselves unable to transfer ideas and strategies from one subject domain to another or from schoolwork activities to fresh learning tasks beyond school.

Many recent projects and curriculum initiatives such as TVEI, LAPP, CDT and GCSE, have emphasised cross-curricular themes to combat compartmentalism; negotiation between teachers and pupils about what should be taught to increase motivation; community links; practical and vocationally-biased activities to enhance relevance; and interactive teaching styles to shift pupils out of passive, recipient roles into active, participatory roles in which thinking, questioning and autonomous learning feature prominently. Above all, the recent initiatives stress the need for increased pupil awareness of problem-solving processes. At last secondary schools are recognising that developing children's conceptual skills and understanding is at least as important as teaching facts and information.

Nevertheless, in spite of this optimistic picture many teachers are ill-equipped to handle these new curriculum demands. Some teachers experience difficulty in developing the kinds of interactive teaching styles necessary for problem-solving work. Others are unable to analyse and articulate the cognitive processes underlying their own subject discipline. Moreover, different school subjects emphasise and expose the need for different problem-solving skills. Of course, some educationalists have argued that teaching particular subjects like maths or Latin can 'train the mind' to learn anything. However, there are few advocates of this view nowadays. Indeed, it is difficult to promote the development of a comprehensive range of cognitive skills and strategies from within one or two subject areas. Notwithstanding these issues, the content demands imposed by the examination system constantly overshadow process considerations.

'Learning to learn' is far too important to be left to the vagaries of recent curriculum trends. There seems to be a need to make cognitive processes far more explicit to both pupils and teachers. To a degree, some of these issues were addressed by the 'study skills' movement. Numerous manuals were produced from 1900 onwards, offering advice on how to teach learning techniques. Unfortunately, the advice given has remained relatively unchanged since the beginning of the century and has lacked any empirical evidence or theoretical basis. It has often been too general to be of use and applied too late, at 16–18 years, when habits and learning routines are already well established.

It is interesting to note that the content-process debate has also been mirrored in the vocational training field; here it is recognised as important not only to impart the knowledge and skills required for a specific job but also to teach the skills and processes which underpin successful performance in many contexts. Accordingly, attempts have been made to apply the study skills philosophy within YTS, as a result of the FEU *How Do I Learn?* Project (Downs and Perry, 1984). This project has produced some creative and interesting ideas, but the constraints imposed by limited training time have meant that many of the ideas in the scheme fall into the 'quick fix' category.

Undoubtedly, the most exciting developments in the learning to learn' field are now arising from practical applications of cognitive psychology. Research has demonstrated that few young adults have acquired efficient learning techniques by the time they leave school. Many individuals, especially those with learning difficulties, cannot explain how they learn, why they fail, or what particular strategies may be appropriate for certain learning tasks. However, there is increasing evidence that individuals *can* be trained in thinking skills, thereby improving their ability to learn. In retrospect, it seems curious that we have invested vast amounts of time and energy in teaching children basic access skills like reading and writing, while paying relatively little attention to consciously developing and extending their range of cognitive skills and strategies. There are some who would argue that this kind of work would amount to teaching intelligence. Others would argue that it involves enabling children to make the best of their intellectual abilities. Either way, the need to teach cognitive skills is crucially important. Any debate should be reserved for the best way of achieving this objective. However, before this can be considered we need to have a clearer understanding of what is meant by 'cognitive' or 'thinking skills'.

2   Thinking skills

What are thinking skills?

'Thinking skills' has become a generic phrase used to encompass many processes involved in learning and problem solving. Naturally, bearing in mind the vast array of very different intellectual tasks, the potential list of processes is infinite. Different researchers and curriculum specialists have emphasised different processes. In an ideal world there would be a universally-agreed taxonomy of cognitive processes, enabling us to identify which processes have the widest currency across many different intellectual tasks. This would enable us to direct our teaching efforts to greatest effect. Unfortunately, there is no such universal agreement. The literature tends to focus on two broad groups of teachable cognitive skills, that we have called: *Cognitive resources* and *Cognitive strategies*.

Cognitive resources

Cognitive resource domains include concepts, essential skills, knowledge and 'tricks of the trade' as well as the verbal tools necessary to name and understand the things we observe, experience and feel. They provide the prerequisites to thinking and problem solving, but the list of items competing for attention is extensive.

Feuerstein *et al* (1979) talk about a list of 'deficient cognitive functions' commonly associated with learning failure. The list appears to be based on clinical experiences and refers to a mixed bag of specific and more general items. The items refer to the 'phase' level of Feuerstein's Cognitive Map. Phase involves an artificial grouping of mental activities into three stages: input

FAILURE TO READ AND INTERPRET
EXPLICIT INSTRUCTIONS

FAILURE TO APPRECIATE THE
NEED FOR PRECISION AND
ACCURACY

POORLY DEVELOPED
CLASSIFICATION SKILLS

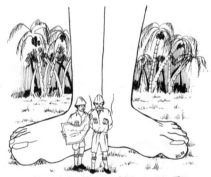

POOR APPRECIATION OF CONVENTIONS
AND REFERENTS IN TIME AND SPACE

(the process of gathering all relevant information); elaboration (efficiently using the information gathered to find solutions); output (executing tasks and communicating findings and solutions both to oneself and others). Examples of impairments at each stage include:

- 'blurred and sweeping perception, lack of or impaired receptive verbal tools that affect discrimination' (*input* phase)
- 'lack of or impaired strategies for hypothesis testing, lack of or impaired planning behaviour' (*elaboration* phase)
- 'trial and error responses, lack of or impaired receptive verbal tools for communicating adequately elaborated responses' (*output* phase)

(For an in-depth appraisal of Feuerstein's Deficient Functions List and his Cognitive Map (Feuerstein *et al*, 1979) see Blagg, Ballinger and Gardner, 1988.) For the purposes of this handbook it is worth recording that Feuerstein's list of common cognitive impairments has been found to be very useful in the classroom, both at the diagnostic level with individual pupils and at the curriculum design level in developing materials to expose and overcome these problems. However, Feuerstein's list is far from exhaustive and individual items cover issues relating to learning style, specific cognitive resources and more general cognitive strategies.

In the interests of clarity we have chosen to separate and expand upon these issues. For the moment we will consider cognitive resources. The Somerset Thinking Skills Course focuses on the domains referred to earlier in this section. Examples of each domain are provided in Table 1. Each of these items could be artificially grouped into the phase sections that Feuerstein refers to.

Deficiencies in these and other basic resources can result in major difficulties in learning and problem solving. At an even more fundamental level, cognitive resource issues underpin actions and performance in many areas of life – as the cartoons illustrate!

There is evidence that many of these essential resources can be taught particularly in relation to specific tasks. However, it is far more difficult to ensure that children achieve purposeful control over them so that when faced with fresh problems they know how to apply them, for instance, when to select and use particular skills and techniques and when to avoid them.

TABLE 1:   **STSC Cognitive resources**

Domains	Examples
A *Concepts*	Colour, number, size, shape, volume, position, time, space, hierarchy, analogy, simile, metaphor
B *Skills and knowledge*	Working precisely and accurately
	Paying close attention to detail
	Recognising and interpreting clues and reference points
	Recognising and interpreting implicit instructions
	Reading and interpreting explicit instructions
	Listening
	Scanning and searching systematically
	Distinguishing relevant from irrelevant information
	Counting and eliminating
	Labelling, coding and abbreviating
	Drawing pictures, diagrams, charts etc
	Understanding universal codes, symbols and conventions
	Recording information in many different modes
	Creating a clear mental picture of objects and events
	Summarising
	Imagining and brainstorming
	Giving clear and appropriate instructions
	Following instructions accurately
	Analysing wholes into parts
	Analysing the stages and sequences in a task
	Synthesising parts into wholes
	Rebuilding, re-assembling, re-organising, re-designing
	Describing, comparing and classifying
	Understanding conventions and referents in time and space
	Understanding the relationship between time and space
	Using spatial and temporal referents in descriptions
	Understanding and using spatial and temporal referents from other people's points of view
	Establishing patterns and relationships enabling predictions in time and space
	Being able to consider differing viewpoints and feelings
	Understanding the nature of bias and prejudice
	Handling several sources of information simultaneously
	Knowing techniques to aid memorising, like visualising, rehearsing, elaborating and mnemonics

Domains	Examples
C *Verbal tools*	Possessing the precise 'verbal tools' to name the things we observe, experience and feel – to allow for: *a* the acquisition of skills, knowledge and concepts. *b* the development and application of cognitive strategies.

Cognitive strategies

Cognitive strategies refer to higher-level general control processes concerned with the selection and coordination of specific cognitive resources for particular purposes. The distinction between cognitive resources and cognitive strategies has been helpfully clarified by Nisbet and Shucksmith (1986) who make a simple analogy with a football team and its trainer. Individual players need to practise many skills, including heading, dribbling, ball control and so on. Prior to a particular match or at half time groups of players may plan certain tactics or strategies which involve a careful selection, sequencing and coordination of skills for a particular purpose. Nisbet and Shucksmith take the analogy further by querying what happens when the strategy does not work. A poor team might continue with the same tactics, irrespective of the outcome. A good team would be able to monitor and assess the situation and flexibly adapt the strategy to achieve the desired goals. It does not matter how proficient the individual players are at particular skills like tackling and sprinting if they cannot coordinate them into useful strategies. Furthermore, the analogy demonstrates that there are different levels of strategic thinking, with monitoring, checking and revising procedures requiring higher-level processes than generating and planning tactics. The problem for the trainer, like the teacher, is that of developing flexible strategic thinkers. While acquiring particular skills and techniques is an important part of educational experience, far more important is the business of developing pupil ability to select and flexibly use these techniques.

As with cognitive resources, various lists of cognitive strategies are utilised by different critical thinking skills programmes and learning to learn courses. Nevertheless, there is much greater consensus about the various domains that are important and the kinds of strategies within them. A fuller discussion of this area is given in Blagg, Ballinger and Gardner (1988). At this stage it is sufficient to say that strategies can be ordered into a hierarchy. Thus, strategies within the domain of recognising and defining problems, or planning, form a continuum with higher-level strategies in the domains of monitoring, self-testing and evaluating. Strategies in these latter areas require more conscious awareness of cognitive processes – an area of self-knowledge referred to in the psychological literature as 'metacognition'.

Metacognitivists like Flavell (1977) and Campione, Brown and Ferrara (1982) argue that if pupils can become more consciously aware of their own thought processes when solving problems, this may in turn lead to better control over these same processes. They note that young children and low achievers are less able than adults or high achievers to talk about techniques and methods of problem solving and learning employed in specific tasks. Thus, curriculum initiatives emphasising active learning methods and problem-solving approaches not only dovetail with recent ideas about the nature of intelligence and learning to learn, but also with views expressed by the metacognitivists. In fact, the design loop familiar in craft, design and technology and other similar problem-solving models featured in investigative maths, science and humanities, overlap considerably with the strategy domains commonly referred to in cognitive psychology. Although the names of each domain often vary, the areas encompassed typically include:

1   Gathering and organising all relevant information
2   Recognising and defining the problem
3   Generating alternative solutions
4   Planning tactics
5   Monitoring performance
6   Checking performance against original aims
7   Revising plans and strategies to meet original aims
8   Evaluating performance and strategies

Curiously, communication is rarely listed as a separate area. Nevertheless, the process of communication does in itself involve a range of strategic issues which parallel those noted in the above list. For instance, as recent reports from the Assessment of Performance Unit (APU) indicate, we need to use different kinds of language in describing, instructing, analysing, hypothesising, evaluating and justifying. Many children do not experience problems in describing, narrating and instructing but do find great difficulty with the more sophisticated functions. We will return to this aspect of the work when talking about developing oracy and managing group work in the *Teacher guidelines* section on page 56.

As we said at the beginning of this section the fundamental issue facing teachers is that of developing flexibility and adaptability in the pupils, ie teaching them to transfer and generalise. Although this area is discussed a great deal in the literature, the terms 'transfer and generalisation' rarely appear in design or problem-solving loops and are typically not mentioned in strategy lists. We do not want pupils simply to become more proficient in a particular problem-solving technique which they can then use with familiar tasks where the teacher is there to prompt and support. The ultimate aim of problem-solving work is to prepare children to handle unfamiliar problems and learning tasks independently. In order to do this they need to be able to transfer and generalise skills, strategies and procedures learnt in particular situations to new contexts. Again the key to this area seems to be metacognition; if pupils are aware of and understand the problem-solving processes involved in many tasks maybe they will be able to recall, select and transfer these processes to similar tasks. At a more sophisticated level, metacognition may lead to pupils identifying common process requirements in very different types of tasks, thereby enabling generalisation. Naturally, we need to consider the strategic issues involved and the teacher's role in promoting this process. Again we will return to this crucial issue in the section on teacher guidelines.

For the purposes of the *Somerset Thinking Skills Course* we have integrated many of the ideas discussed under the cognitive strategies heading into a problem-solving loop (Figure 2.1). Readers will note that 'Communication' and 'Transfer and generalisation' are included in the strategy loop. While the diagram implies a natural sequence, numbers and directional arrows have been omitted in recognition of the fact that real-life problem solving is rarely a straightforward, unidirectional sequence. For instance, we may reach the planning stage and then find we need to go back and gather more information before continuing. At the monitoring and checking stage, we may discover that our solution strategy is quite inappropriate, forcing us to completely re-think our ideas. Each of the strategy domains referred to in the diagram is expanded in Table 2.

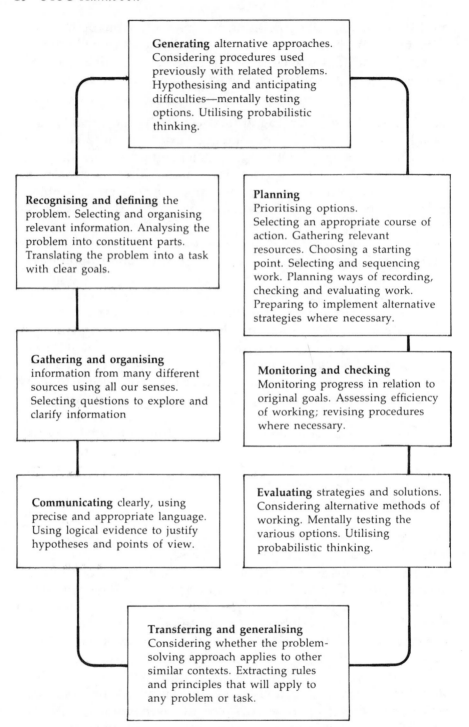

Generating alternative approaches. Considering procedures used previously with related problems. Hypothesising and anticipating difficulties—mentally testing options. Utilising probabilistic thinking.

Recognising and defining the problem. Selecting and organising relevant information. Analysing the problem into constituent parts. Translating the problem into a task with clear goals.

Planning
Prioritising options.
Selecting an appropriate course of action. Gathering relevant resources. Choosing a starting point. Selecting and sequencing work. Planning ways of recording, checking and evaluating work. Preparing to implement alternative strategies where necessary.

Gathering and organising information from many different sources using all our senses. Selecting questions to explore and clarify information

Monitoring and checking
Monitoring progress in relation to original goals. Assessing efficiency of working; revising procedures where necessary.

Communicating clearly, using precise and appropriate language. Using logical evidence to justify hypotheses and points of view.

Evaluating strategies and solutions. Considering alternative methods of working. Mentally testing the various options. Utilising probabilistic thinking.

Transferring and generalising
Considering whether the problem-solving approach applies to other similar contexts. Extracting rules and principles that will apply to any problem or task.

FIGURE 2.1   STSC PROBLEM-SOLVING LOOP

TABLE 2: **STSC Cognitive strategies**

Domains	Examples
A *Gathering and organising*	Gathering and interpreting information from many different sources using all our senses Selecting questions to explore and clarify any explicit information Selecting questions to explore and clarify 'disguised' or implicit information
B *Recognising and defining*	Clarifying the problem by comparing with previous experiences Deciding upon additional information required to clarify the problem Analysing the problem into its constituent parts Translating the problem into a task with clear goals Visualising the task Deciding on the main steps involved in the task Selecting and organising relevant information Developing a system to check that all relevant information is gathered and remembered
C *Generating*	Generating alternative options Considering procedures used previously with related problems Generating alternative (simplified or analogous) related problems that can help to clarify the procedure required Hypothesising and mentally testing various options Anticipating the probable outcomes of various courses of action
D *Planning*	Prioritising options Selecting an appropriate course of action Choosing a starting point Selecting a sequence of working Planning a way of recording and monitoring work and progress Developing ways of checking work eg repeating the same procedure; reversing the order of working; using an appropriate alternative procedure Planning ways of evaluating methods of working, eg considering whether: the solution fits the original aims of the task; the procedure was efficient; a more efficient procedure was available; the approach can be used in solving other problems Preparing to implement alternative strategies where necessary

Domains	Examples
E *Monitoring and checking*	Monitoring progress in relation to original goals
	Assessing efficiency (accuracy and speed) of working in relation to original goals
	Revising procedures and plans in the light of feedback from working on the task
	Implementing alternative strategies where necessary
F *Evaluating*	Considering:
	• was the task adequately defined?
	• was enough information collected?
	• was the procedure chosen appropriate to the goals?
	Reflecting on alternative routes/options to achieve the same goal
	Considering the efficiency of available alternatives
	Mentally testing the various options
G *Transferring and generalising*	Exploring ways in which objects, events, problems and experiences can be inter-related
	Considering whether:
	• the problem-solving approach applies to other contexts (transfer);
	• there are any lessons that can be learned from the activities (inductive reasoning);
	• any rules and principles can be derived from the activity (inductive reasoning);
	• the rules and principles derived from the task can be applied to other problems/tasks (deductive reasoning).
	Dealing in probabilities – making 'guesstimates' – hypothesising and predicting about related problems/issues
H *Communicating*	Selecting appropriate communication mode(s), eg diagrammatic, pictorial and verbal, to suit the audience and the situation
	Selecting the appropriate language to:
	• describe objects, events and situations;
	• compare objects, events and situations;
	• convey information in a way that is clearly understood and socially acceptable to the audience;
	• recall and recount information and experiences;
	• give instructions;
	• analyse the way something works or the way it is made;
	• explain how, why, what, where and when;
	• hypothesise and anticipate;
	• speculate on alternatives and probabilities;
	• evaluate evidence;
	• justify a viewpoint with logical evidence.

FAILURE TO RECOGNISE AND DEFINE THE PROBLEM

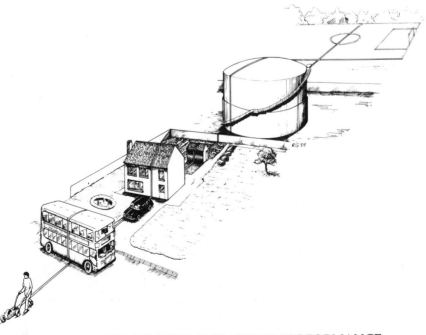

FAILURE TO MONITOR AND CHECK PERFORMANCE

Learning styles, attitudes and beliefs

The notion of learning styles and learning approaches is also subsumed under the generic phrase, 'thinking skills'. Both style and approach to learning are closely related to attitudes, beliefs and motivational issues. The two terms mean something rather different but both are worthy of consideration.

Nisbet and Shucksmith (1986) regard learning approach as a central overriding control strategy. These authors quote Brown's (1974) work on children with learning difficulties. Brown concludes that the most fundamental strategic issue characterising children with learning problems is a lack of any intention to make a plan. If the children were instructed to make a plan they could often perform satisfactorily. However, they rarely engaged in planning behaviour spontaneously. Brown terms this willingness to engage in planning behaviour – 'planfulness'.

The extent to which children are active, optimistic and purposeful in their approach to learning tasks is likely to be linked with previous learning experiences. The child who has been constantly criticised or has experienced continual failure may have developed poor self-esteem, leading to diminished expectations of success. Denis Lawrence's (1988) handbook for teachers on *Enhancing self-esteem in the classroom*, is a useful source of ideas for bringing about changes in this area. The child who has been over-protected and never encouraged or allowed to work independently may well have learned to be helpless. This type of child is unlikely to spontaneously apply strategies but rather will wait for adult guidance. The child who has never established a consistent and positive connection between effort and achievement may feel that learning is a result of influences beyond his control. This type of child may feel that it is not worth making an effort because it rarely pays off. Furthermore, successful performance on a task is likely to be attributed to 'good luck' rather than any factor that the child has some responsibility for. It seems likely that a history of successful learning experiences in which the child feels responsible for his or her success is a necessary, although not sufficient, condition for strategic thinking.

It is a common experience for children with learning problems to be told to 'try harder'. Frequently this does not result in greater success. Many children implicitly or explicitly receive the message that they lack ability. Some teachers try to combat feelings of inadequacy by counselling the pupils to feel pleased about every small step they take in learning and problem solving, even if it involves an enormous effort. There is also the tendency to simplify learning tasks or even remove children from challenging opportunities to problem solve, in order to protect them from the discomfort and self-deprecation associated with failure. While there may be certain circumstances that require the cautious use of these approaches, they can often result in self-fulfilling prophecies. A much more appropriate approach, in tune with the philosophy of STSC, would be to help the child to appreciate that learning or problem-solving difficulties are the result of a failure to know about or apply certain cognitive strategies. This way of working involves the teacher in analysing the kinds of cognitive strategies and resources required by particular problems or tasks. The approach is more optimistic as it communicates to the child that strategies can be learned and that examining failure is a very positive way of learning to learn.

Stott (1976) refers to the child's cognitive style as a crucial factor affecting the ability to learn. He describes the 'unforthcoming' individual as one who lacks confidence in coping with new tasks and unfamiliar situations. This sort of child typically adopts the role of someone less able, rather than risk the possibility of failure. The child is typically unresponsive in class discussions and may generally appear to lack initiative. However, once familiar with the expected task such children can show increased confidence and normal competence.

Stott also refers to the 'inconsequential' child who acts impulsively without any anticipation or mental rehearsal of behaviour. Learning tasks are performed on a trial and error or 'guesswork' basis. The child rarely invests sufficient time and energy in recognising and defining problems, planning solutions and methods of working before acting. The impulsive person is one who is often in conflict with authority for acting without thinking.

Impulsivity has been the subject of considerable description and research (Kagan, Rosman, Day, Albert and Phillips, 1964). It has been linked with poor academic performance and is regarded by many as being one of the prime reasons for learning failure. Consequently, most cognitive intervention programmes strongly emphasise the need to inhibit the child's first thoughts and responses and to promote in the child a more reflective, cautious approach when faced with problems. Feuerstein's *Instrumental Enrichment Programme* emphasises this strongly with the slogan, 'Just a minute, let me think'.

There have been many other studies exploring learning style and linking it with general attitudes and approaches to tasks across many different contexts. Different researchers have identified different styles although many of their findings overlap. For instance, Witkin's (1977) notions on 'field dependent/independent' persons (later referred to as those with more 'articulated' versus 'global' learning styles) connects with Kagan's impulsive/reflective continuum. In reality, different types of tasks and problems with different contexts demand different types of approaches. Some types of situations lend themselves to more holistic, global learning styles where risk taking is acceptable. Other situations require a more reflective style with cautious, analytic and systematic methods of working. The use of many different types of task within STSC enables the teacher to mediate for increased reflectivity where necessary, whilst offering opportunities for encouraging quicker and less cautious responses from those individuals who are already too analytic, focused and over-anxious about making mistakes.

The learning styles debate provides an important orientation for teachers in that there does seem to be evidence that children commonly use preferred styles of working irrespective of the problem or the context. Consistent attention within STSC to the selection of appropriate cognitive resources and strategies for particular problems should address this issue.

Summary

In summary, there are many factors influencing children's willingness and ability to think strategically. Many children have a very limited repertoire of strategies and keep to the same old routines irrespective of whether they are successful or not. Some children have quite a wide strategic repertoire but still lack the ability to select the appropriate ways of working for fresh learning tasks. We have discussed a number of issues relating to attitudes, beliefs and motivation that need to be addressed. At the same time, we have emphasised that many cognitive resource prerequisites underpin the main problem-solving domains. These prerequisites need to be identified, assessed and taught where necessary.

Issues relating to attitudes, beliefs, learning styles and approaches, cognitive strategies and cognitive resources all interact in varied ways in different children, adding to the complexities of under-

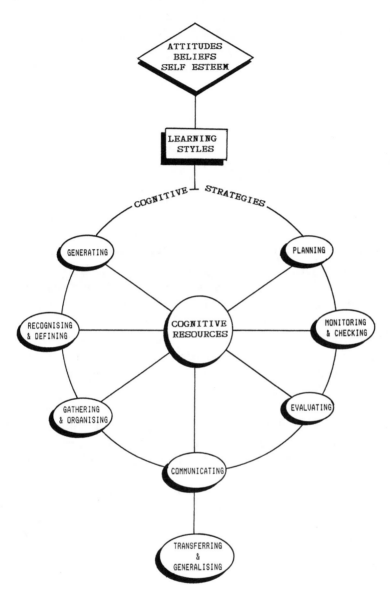

FIGURE 2.2   STSC WORKING MODEL

standing and positively intervening in children's cognitive growth. The pupil activities within STSC have been developed to enable teachers to expose and work with many of these issues, and the related guidelines explain the important areas involved in each pupil activity. A summative diagram of the main domains covered in STSC is shown in Figure 2.2.

3 Teaching intelligence

Cognitive skills programmes

In the USA there are now numerous cognitive skills programmes that claim to provide the materials to teach various component processes involved in intellectual tasks. Lipman's *Philosophy for Children* (Lipman, Sharp and Oscanyon, 1980), De Bono's (1973) *CORT Lateral Thinking Programme* and *The Chicago Mastery Skills Programme* (Chicago Board of Education, 1980) are particularly well known. In recent years, Sternberg has been developing his own new techniques for assessing intelligence and teaching critical thinking skills. There is considerable overlap between many of these programmes, although they each emphasise different strategies and resources, with some being more comprehensive than others. We have reviewed and compared a number of these programmes elsewhere (Blagg, Ballinger and Gardner, 1988). Undoubtedly, the cognitive intervention programme which has attracted most attention and has been subject to most research is Feuerstein's *Instrumental Enrichment*. As our work has developed out of the experience of using IE it will be helpful if we briefly describe the programme at this point.

Instrumental Enrichment

The *Instrumental Enrichment Programme* consists of 15 instruments (units) each made up of a series of paper and pencil tasks that provide the basis of a one-hour teaching session, conducted three to five times a week over a two to three year period. The programme is accompanied by a highly detailed teacher's manual.

Each instrument focuses on particular mental skills and provides opportunities for the teacher to teach the prerequisite skills for thinking and learning. Fundamental activities like thinking

24

carefully before acting; developing systematic strategies; comparing; searching for patterns and relationships are central to the whole programme. Pupils are not only encouraged to think before acting but are also asked to think about their own thinking – 'What was the best way of solving the problem? Could you have used another route? What makes that solution or way better than another?'

The tasks are highly abstract and devoid of familiar subject content, containing ideas and materials more consistent with psychological aptitude and ability tests. The tasks within each instrument start at a very simple level but become more and more complex with the basic concepts and skills being introduced in increasingly demanding contexts. At a critical stage in each instrument a 'mastery' page is introduced that summarises and confirms the pupils' growing competence whilst checking for any residual difficulties. The emphasis is on the process of thinking rather than the acquisition of knowledge. A crucial feature of each lesson is the involvement of pupils and teacher in 'bridging' activities, whereby pupils are encouraged to find relationships between the strategies used on the abstract materials and applications to real life – in other words, *transfer and generalisation*.

Evaluating Instrumental Enrichment

IE has attracted considerable international attention from psychologists and educationalists. The programme has been applied to many different age and ability groups and has been subjected to more rigorous evaluation than any other cognitive skills programme. Major evaluations have been carried out in Israel, Canada, Venezuela, USA and England. The research findings are optimistic but they do not unequivocally endorse the claims made for the programme, particularly with respect to transfer and generalisation. This does not necessarily undermine the claims for IE, but rather points up the complexities of the research. These issues are comprehensively reviewed in Blagg, Ballinger and Gardner (1988).

In England a consortium of five LEAs explored the viability of the materials for secondary pupils, under the supervision of the Schools' Council. The project looked especially at training, staffing and timetabling problems as well as individual reactions by teachers and pupils. The final report (Weller and Craft, 1984) was cautiously positive and highlighted the need for more exploratory work and rigorous evaluation. Since then a number of LEAs have established independent evaluations of IE.

In September 1983 Somerset obtained substantial funding under the auspices of The Low Attaining Pupil Project with a large proportion of the budget allocated to investigate the application of IE to 14–16 year old low-achieving adolescents in four Bridgwater secondary schools. Over a three-year period approximately 1000 pupils were exposed to IE and about 30 teachers and three psychologists were trained in the programme. Eight of the group became qualified as local trainers in IE and four have obtained further training in Israel. Over a two-year period 250 children and 30 teachers were closely monitored as part of a rigorous evaluation of IE (Blagg, 1984). The detailed findings are reported in Blagg (1988) and Blagg, Ballinger and Gardner (1988).

A summary of the Somerset research findings

There were many practical problems in implementing IE in mainstream secondary schools. The degree of support for the programme varied from school to school and the timetabling arrangements were less than ideal. Furthermore, teacher interpretation of the programme varied enormously as a result of many factors including the amount of training and experience in using the programme, the number of years of teaching experience and the degree of support and encouragement available in each school.

The pupils

An initial analysis considering all of the IE pupils together, compared with the controls, showed some minor positive trends favouring the IE pupils, but not sufficiently marked to reach statistical significance. However, within the experimental group there was enormous variability in pupil outcome. Some groups in more supportive schools, whose teachers demonstrated a better understanding of the programme, produced significant and worthwhile cognitive and behavioural gains in the pupils.

A special rating scale was designed for monitoring changes in classroom behaviour over time (Blagg, 1984). It was possible to use this scale on a small sample of the IE pupils to obtain measures of classroom behaviour at the beginning and end of the programme. Within the IE class it was noted that IE pupils became significantly more:

- self-disciplined in class;
- active contributors to class discussions;

- inclined to listen to other pupils' comments in class discussions;
- inclined to defend their own opinions on the basis of logical evidence;
- able to describe to other pupils a number of different strategies for solving problems;
- likely to spontaneously read and follow instructions carefully before starting on a task;
- able to handle two or more sources of information simultaneously when solving problems;
- able to make spontaneous relationships between ideas and principles in different curriculum areas.

All the pupils were individually interviewed at the beginning and end of the study. Many of the teacher observations were confirmed by pupils' comments about their own behaviour and feelings. For instance, pupils commonly said that prior to IE lessons they had never wanted to contribute willingly to class discussions. Many pupils talked about acquiring new words and, more importantly, about utilising the ideas lying behind the words.

> I've learnt a lot of new words. I don't use them in other lessons much but I do use the ideas. For instance, I never used to *plan* anything or *anticipate* problems. Nowadays, I always think things through. At the weekends I have different plans and *alternatives* in case things don't work out as I think they will.

Qualitative impressions of individual pupils suggested that some were able to generalise from the IE programme to other settings. However, it was not possible to quantify the range and extent of generalisation. Furthermore, no conclusive quantitative evidence was established to show that the behavioural changes observed in IE classes transferred to other classroom settings.

The teachers

Teacher effects were more consistent and impressive. A combination of findings from teacher interviews, classroom observations and attitudinal scales administered at the beginning and end of the study pointed up the importance and potential of cognitive skills work. For many teachers, involvement with Feuerstein's ideas generated more careful thought and analysis about the nature of teaching and the process of learning than any other in-service training programme had hitherto achieved. The relevance of Feuerstein's ideas was for some teachers underlined by an awareness of their own problems in managing certain aspects of the IE programme and the kind of processes they needed to go through to correct their own misconceptions. For many teachers this was quite a humbling experience that gave them insight into pupil learning processes (Blagg, 1988).

The business of grappling with IE was intellectually demanding so that there was often a time lag of one or two years before teachers felt sufficiently conversant with the programme to use it flexibly and apply the principles to their own subject disciplines. Nevertheless, after this ingestion period, the majority of teachers were reporting a number of changes in their attitudes and teaching style. Statistically significant changes were noted amongst the IE teachers concerning their views of themselves as teachers, as expressed on an attitudinal scale administered pre- and post-IE. During the two-year study the IE teachers reported

- greater satisfaction from teaching;
- increased confidence in their teaching ability;
- an increased commitment to teaching;
- a feeling of greater competence in being able to make a valuable contribution to teaching;
- an increased preference for a less directive and more informal approach to teaching;
- an increase in their ability to arouse pupil interest.

There were no similar significant positive attitudinal trends in the control teachers. There was, however, one significant negative trend suggesting that the control teachers became less committed to teaching during the two-year study.

Over the same period positive attitudinal shifts were also noted in the IE teachers with respect to their views concerning the characteristics of low attaining pupils. Statistically significant positive trends were noted indicating an increased feeling that low attainers:

- often have good but unrealised intellectual ability;
- are very capable of thinking for themselves;
- are perfectly capable of generalising what they have learnt;
- are far more capable than most teachers realise;

- can maintain high levels of interest for long periods;
- are very capable of holding good classroom discussions.

Corresponding attitudinal shifts did not occur in the control teachers. In fact the control teachers became more negative over the same period. Two statistically significant negative trends were noted, showing an increased feeling that low attainers:

- usually lack intellectual ability;
- provide little satisfaction for the teacher.

The positive shifts in attitude recorded on the two questionnaires were substantiated by anecdotal comments from the teachers and a number of their colleagues. Teachers became increasingly conscious of their own responsibility for the children's progress. They commented on their change in teaching style, with an increased tendency to adopt a problem-solving approach not only in IE but in their own main subject specialism. In connection with this the use of open-ended rather than closed questioning techniques became more common; teachers moved away from questions requiring a 'yes', 'no' or specific answer in favour of questions leading to many alternative responses. Increasingly IE teachers were observed to be taking more interest in unusual and, at first sight, inappropriate pupil responses – asking pupils to 'say more' rather than ignoring or dismissing the response. Allowing pupils more time to think about and explain their ideas often revealed fascinating insights into pupil understanding, leading to a better 'cognitive match' between the teacher's model of the world and that of the pupils.

At the curriculum level IE teachers became more aware of the process demands involved in many of the initiatives currently underway in our secondary schools. Perhaps more importantly IE teachers were able to experiment with process-orientated teaching without being constrained by the product demands of the normal curriculum. Thus, the more successful teachers were able to provide paradigms of the classroom mechanics and techniques necessary for interactive problem-solving approaches to learning.

Transfer and generalisation

In spite of these highly encouraging findings there were also consistent concerns about the IE programme, especially over the familiar problem of transfer and generalisation. The IE programme offers children a series of novel, abstract activities in a contextually bare medium, freed from traditional subject constraints, which offers the potential for maximum generalisation. The teacher is encouraged to facilitate this process via 'bridging'. In the early stages the teacher needs to provide plenty of examples in which the rules and principles extracted from the abstract activities are applied to other problems and fresh learning situations. Eventually, it is hoped, pupils will make spontaneous generalisations of their own. As noted earlier, there was evidence of this happening in some pupils. However, in many instances both pupils and teachers found it difficult to generalise from abstract contexts to real life. Pupils undoubtedly became more competent in tasks like searching for geometric shapes in amorphous clouds of dots. Unfortunately, the skills and strategies exposed by these abstract tasks often remained steadfastly tied to those specific contexts. In other words, some pupils and teachers were 'stuck in the dots and triangles'!

This observation may come as no surprise to those who have argued that teaching thinking skills is best achieved by using familiar, everyday contexts. Nevertheless, the latter approach has just as many problems. There is good evidence that working with more familiar and more concrete materials results in many children being unable to generalise from particular examples to new contexts. In other words they get 'stuck in the concrete'! For instance, analytic principles learnt in chemistry do not necessarily generalise to history or English lessons. Children often exhibit what Feuerstein calls an 'episodic grasp of reality' in which learning is experienced in unrelated discrete packets of information.

General concerns

Apart from worries about transfer and generalisation, the IE teachers were concerned about a range of practical and theoretical issues more fully discussed elsewhere (Blagg, Ballinger and Gardner, 1988). Concerns included worries about the cost of training and materials; the repetitive nature and presentation of the materials; and the lack of any clear links in the programme with other curriculum areas. The teacher's manual was complicated to use and the ideas contained in it were not linked to Feuerstein's mediated learning experience parameters. In other words, the technical aspects of the programme were covered but very little explanation was given about the kinds of teacher behaviours necessary to achieve the goals of the programme.

Summary

In summary, the implementation of Feuerstein's *Instrumental Enrichment Programme* combined with a detailed analysis of his theories and beliefs has pointed up the potential of cognitive skills work and exposed many important issues at the heart of 'learning to learn'. The principles and ideas in the programme have much to offer with respect to enhancing more positive teacher attitudes and facilitating a more interactive process-orientated approach to teaching. Nevertheless, IE's abstract format does have major drawbacks for pupils, teachers and the mainstream school curriculum. It is for these reasons that the *Somerset Thinking Skills Course* was produced, piloted and published.

4 The Somerset Thinking Skills Course

We have produced a set of materials specifically designed for classroom use, as a direct outcome of the practical experience of using Feuerstein's more clinical programme. Naturally, some of the goals and theoretical principles of STSC overlap with Feuerstein's original work. At the same time, many other theoretical and curricular influences have affected the final shape and style of our programme.

Details of the working model underpinning STSC have been discussed earlier (page 2). Readers may like to revisit this section when considering the general aims of STSC recorded in Figure 4.1. The teacher guidelines for each module explain how the teacher can realise these eight aims. An introduction to the style and format of the teacher guidelines is provided in a later section (page 56).

Structure and organisation of pupil activities within each module

Like IE, the *Somerset Thinking Skills Course* consists of a series of visually based materials which serve as springboards for each lesson. The materials are arranged in modules around themes in much the same way as IE, although the themes in the two programmes do not entirely correspond. Whereas IE tends to focus almost exclusively on reducing impulsivity and overcoming 'deficient functions', STSC concerns itself with wider issues of learning style and cognitive strategy as well as the cognitive resources underlying these areas.

In *Instrumental Enrichment* the majority of the tasks are highly abstract. The repetition within each instrument tends to reduce

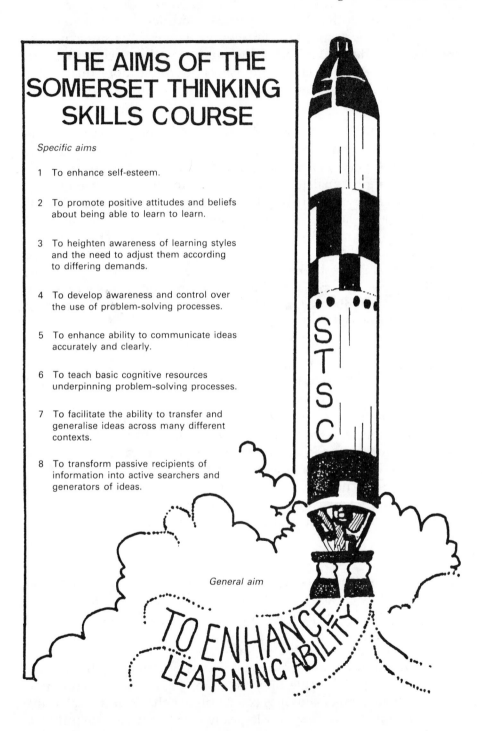

THE AIMS OF THE SOMERSET THINKING SKILLS COURSE

Specific aims

1   To enhance self-esteem.

2   To promote positive attitudes and beliefs about being able to learn to learn.

3   To heighten awareness of learning styles and the need to adjust them according to differing demands.

4   To develop awareness and control over the use of problem-solving processes.

5   To enhance ability to communicate ideas accurately and clearly.

6   To teach basic cognitive resources underpinning problem-solving processes.

7   To facilitate the ability to transfer and generalise ideas across many different contexts.

8   To transform passive recipients of information into active searchers and generators of ideas.

General aim

TO ENHANCE LEARNING ABILITY

FIGURE 4.1 SOMERSET THINKING SKILLS COURSE GENERAL & SPECIFIC AIMS.

the emphasis on the need to recognise and define problems in all but the earlier activities. Furthermore, the consistent use of particular modes and styles of presentation within each instrument offers relatively little chance to assess anything more than 'close transfer' of skills within the programme and can lead to boredom for some pupils.

In contrast, STSC offers a wider range of activities and contexts within each modular theme. This provides greater novelty, encouraging and maintaining interest and motivation. It also results in a more consistent emphasis on problem solving generally. The pupils are constantly required to recognise and define different types of tasks and to generate, monitor and evaluate different methods of working. In addition, the wide variation in the activities provides the opportunity both to assess and to encourage transfer of skills and strategies across more 'distanced' situations. Further, the use of some more naturalistic problem-solving situations and discussion tasks stimulates the generalisation of skills and ideas to fresh contexts.

Teachers will notice that some of the STSC tasks are open ended in that they are open to many possible interpretations and do not have prescribed 'correct' answers. Other tasks are more focused and closed and do require specific solutions. In either case, emphasis is placed upon children being able to justify their interpretations and to evaluate and communicate clearly their solutions and methods of working. Whether the tasks are open or closed, we have deliberately made much use of ambiguity. Many of the tasks do not have written explicit instructions. Those that do, still require very careful interpretation as well as close attention to many implicit instructions. There are a number of reasons for this:

1   We wish to break down the familiar pupil expectation that they will be told exactly what to do. From the early stages of the work pupils are required to think for themselves in defining the tasks.
2   Use of ambiguity allows for many justifiable interpretations, prompting much debate and discussion amongst the pupils.
3   The range of viable interpretations provokes close attention to detail and encourages comparative behaviour in evaluating the most adequate and logically consistent task definitions.
4   It reduces impulsivity by communicating to the pupils that the tasks are rarely straightforward and have to be thought through.

5   It gradually encourages many more reticent pupils to risk a contribution in group or class discussion work, in the knowledge that teacher is not looking for set answers to the tasks.

6   It sharpens pupil awareness of the need for precision and accuracy in many everyday communications to avoid unintended ambiguity. It is interesting to note that children who come from families where ambiguous communications are noticed and challenged from an early age, develop better language skills than those whose parents regularly give and receive confusing messages without question.

7   It encourages pupils to 'read between the lines' when faced with any kind of problem, ie it establishes a routine wherein the child searches for implicit clues and information and for what is not implied as well as analysing the obvious details. This is an important aspect of successful academic performance. Many children fail in examinations because they have not appreciated the subtleties of the questions. More importantly than this, everyday interactions with peers, family and others require us to recognise, interpret and manage ambiguity, noticing for instance disparity between someone's body language and/or tone of voice and the content of their message.

Thus within each module there are open-ended and closed tasks of varying complexity, presented in different modes. These tasks can be separated into three types: *Stimulus activities, Artificial tasks* and *Naturalistic tasks*. We will consider each of these in turn.

Stimulus activites

Stimulus activities establish a meaningful context and theme as a backcloth to the rest of the activities in each module. Moreover, they broaden pupil learning by offering numerous opportunities to explore connections and associations between many different areas of experience that may otherwise remain unrelated. The stimulus materials are quite complex and in themselves pose particular kinds of problems that require particular styles of strategic thinking. They are designed as open-ended activities that foster and encourage imaginative and divergent interpretations with the proviso that they can be justified by reference to the information provided. In general this type of activity is intended to develop confidence and to facilitate small group and class discussion work, promoting oracy skills and shared working. An example of this type of activity is shown in Figure 4.2.

This introductory stimulus page shows a picture of a living room with many people involved in various activities. There are no explicit instructions but the bottom frame shows cartoon figures that provide a key to understanding the nature and purpose of the activity. There are many ways in which this activity can be used. For instance, pupils can be helped to scan the main picture

FIGURE 4.2 'THE LIVING ROOM'
(from *Foundations for problem solving*)

and the key frame before being put into groups to consider questions like, *What is the main picture all about? What does the key frame represent? What is the relationship betwen the two?* The task is intended to motivate pupils to explore the ways in which we obtain information from one or more of our senses. It offers the opportunity of considering a wide range of related issues, eg the use of technology to heighten sensory information; communication (or lack of it) in the picture; the effects of losing one or more of our senses.

The cartoons in the bottom frame depict the usual five senses (touching, seeing, smelling, tasting and hearing) but in addition, there are two more ambiguous background figures. One could be taken to represent the '6th' sense (in common usage, intuition, ESP or in the psychological world, the monitoring of one's bodily processes like hunger and emotion). The other could be interpreted as the '7th' sense (in common usage – thinking, imagining or, in the psychological world, 'metacognition' – the conscious awareness of one's own thoughts and problem-solving processes, knowing why you are succeeding or why you are failing).

The activity is open ended and full of intentionally ambiguous detail to encourage pupils to share ideas and recognise the diversity of justifiable interpretations.

Artificial tasks

The artificial tasks have a similar purpose to activities in the IE programme, being designed to expose, teach and offer practice in particular cognitive resources (concepts, vocabulary, skills and conventions). Here, however, the use of many different tasks in varying modes offers the teacher the opportunity of exploring the extent to which resources learned in one context are spontaneously transferred to a range of related but different contexts. The STSC materials also lend themselves to more interactive forms of learning than the IE materials in that many of the artificial tasks have been designed for paired and group work rather than solely independent work. Some of the tasks are 'closed' and require a very focused, serialistic approach to find one particular solution; other tasks are more 'open ended' and ambiguous, with many alternative interpretations and solutions. The open-ended tasks require pupils to make assumptions about the meanings of the tasks and to analyse the basis of their assumptions. Figure 4.3 illustrates a 'closed' artificial task.

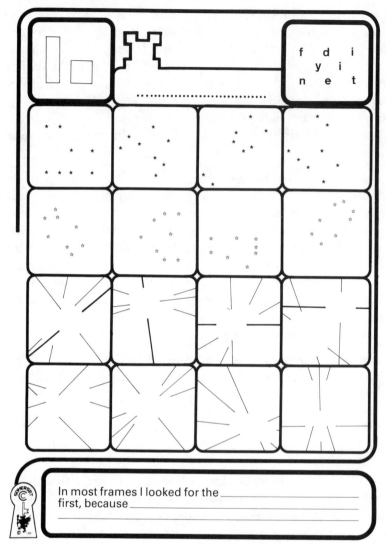

FIGURE 4.3   ABSTRACT SEARCH TASK E
(from *Foundations for problem solving*)

This example is taken from a series of highly abstract search tasks
that become increasingly complex as the programme progresses.
In the early stages, various conventions are established. Thus,
pupils will recognise that the top left emphasised frame illustrates
two model figures that can be found in exactly the same size and
form in each of the subsequent 16 frames. The stars and the tips
of the lines in the later frames are used to construct the corners
of the model figures. The shapes may overlap or change in
orientation. However, the first frame (1.1) always allows for the

model figures to be reproduced in exactly the same position as shown in the model frame.

The top right emphasised frame forms part of an up-turned key and contains an anagram (strategy) which emphasises key vocabulary associated with the programme and the task itself. The dotted line provides space for the pupils to record the correct version of the anagram. The small frame at the bottom of the page contains a cloze procedure activity prompting pupils to discuss strategic issues related to the more difficult frames.

Naturalistic tasks

The inclusion of more naturalistic tasks within each STSC module enables the teacher to check for spontaneous transfer of cognitive resources to problem-solving situations that simulate real life experiences. In these tasks the pupils need to apply a comprehensive range of problem-solving strategies which in turn are dependent upon the possession of certain cognitive resources. Pupil difficulties with these naturalistic problem-solving tasks offer the teacher the chance to mediate at a macro and a micro level. Some pupils can demonstrate knowledge of numerous cognitive resources but remain unable to select and deploy them in appropriate problem-solving contexts. In contrast, other pupils may experience strategic difficulties because they still have major gaps in their cognitive resources requiring intensive help. Figure 4.4 illustrates a naturalistic task.

This open-ended activity presents a familiar type of problem-solving situation. The main picture shows a woman who has lost her key and is locked out of the house. The pupils are implicitly required to consider alternative options and decide the most appropriate actions to take according to the four situations depicted in the bottom frame. The activity lends itself to small group work enabling comparison of different solutions generated to deal with the various scenarios. Generalisation issues include the need to consider consequences before selecting actions appropriate to circumstances. The activity offers the teacher the opportunity of assessing pupil ability to transfer strategies and resources used in earlier pages.

In summary, teachers should note that within each module the difficulty level of pupil activities is gradually increased by making the tasks either more abstract (more removed from concrete experiences with greater use of symbolism) and/or more complex

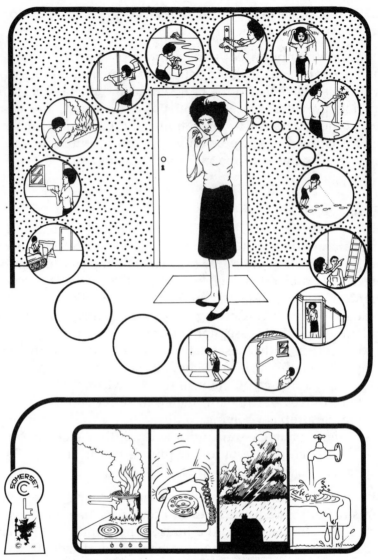

FIGURE 4.4   'THE LOST KEY'
(from *Foundations for problem solving*)

(involving greater amounts of information from many different sources). Each task uses a mixture of different styles and modes of presentation (pictorial, numerical, diagrammatic, verbal. . .). The tasks can be broadly grouped into *stimulus*, *artificial* and *naturalistic* activities. However, some involve elements from one or more of these categories. We can express this visually as shown in Figure 4.5. Here, the square represents stimulus activities, the circle depicts artificial tasks and the triangle naturalistic tasks. The concentric shapes within each of these areas represent the different levels of difficulty.

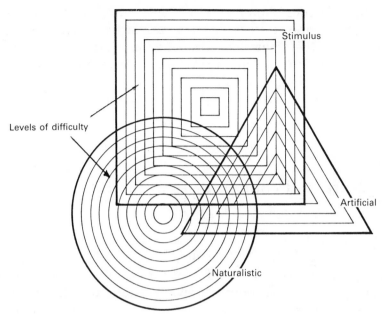

FIGURE 4.5   THE RELATIONSHIP BETWEEN LEVELS OF
DIFFICULTY AND TYPES OF ACTIVITY WITHIN EACH MODULE

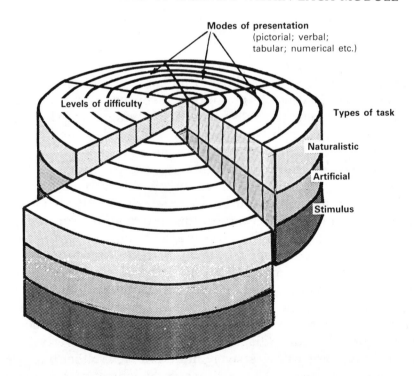

FIGURE 4.6   THE ORGANISATION AND STRUCTURE OF
ACTIVITIES WITHIN EACH STSC MODULE.

Figure 4.6 provides another way of representing the relationship between the various features of each pupil activity within any one module. Here, the diagram can be taken to represent a section of tree trunk in which the concentric rings indicate the varying levels of difficulty, the slices depict different modes and the different layers of the trunk represent types of task (stimulus, artificial and naturalistic).

The nature and content of each module

The modules within STSC have been organised to suit a spiralling linear model graded in difficulty. Each module revisits and builds on ideas, principles and strategies established earlier and continually checks for pupil knowledge and use of important cognitive resources. There are eight modules in the complete course although additional ones may be added later.

1 *Foundations for problem solving*

This is the first module in the course, which sets the scene for all subsequent modules. It establishes the aims of the course and its meaning and relevance to the pupils. It concentrates on reducing impulsivity, developing self-esteem, improving oracy skills, and fostering the ability to work independently and in small groups – enabling the teacher to establish the right kind of working environment for learning to learn. The module places a heavy emphasis on the early stages of any problem-solving process, highlighting important resources and strategies involved in gathering and organising relevant information and recognising and defining problems. Pupils are encouraged to recognise and analyse implicit as well as explicit information; to generate and select strategies for working on the different tasks; and to develop systems for recording and checking information. The need to hypothesise and deal in probabilities is inherent in many of the activities. In common with later modules, a variety of modes is used (pictorial, figural, diagrammatic, numerical and verbal) with activities becoming progressively more complex so that pupils are increasingly encouraged to handle several sources of information simultaneously.

2 *Analysing and synthesising*

This module develops important vocabulary, concepts, skills and strategies introduced in the *Foundations* module but focuses more specifically on the nature of analysis and synthesis and applications to everyday life. As in the previous module, the materials include increasingly difficult overlapping stimulus, artificial and naturalistic tasks that develop pupil understanding of part-whole relationships in both structures and operations. The final stages of the module lead on to an appreciation of the interrelationship between structure, function and aesthetic/cultural considerations.

"Has sir been waiting long?"

POOR TEMPORAL AWARENESS

3   *Positions in time and space*

This third module heightens pupil awareness of the way in which temporal and spatial considerations lie at the heart of planning and anticipating. The module exposes and integrates key concepts and vocabulary relating to reference points in time and space. Analytic behaviour is now enhanced with specific spatial labelling systems and given a past-present-future dimension.

4   *Comparative thinking*

Comparative thinking focuses on the distinction between describing and comparing before developing the nature, meaning and purpose of comparison utilising a wide variety of contexts and problem-solving situations. It explores the contribution spontaneous comparative behaviour makes to all kinds of decision making. The later stages of the module demonstrate how comparison forms the basis of classification. The nature and purpose of classification is explored and related in a variety of ways to both subject matter and social organisations.

5   *Understanding analogies*

This module follows on naturally from *Comparative thinking*. It shows how analogy, metaphor and simile can all be reduced to a sequence of comparisons. The module begins with a series of tasks centring around different types of transformations (pictorial, figural and cartoon) requiring careful comparative behaviour. It then goes on to show how transformations form the basis of understanding different kinds of analogies. The role of analogy, simile and metaphor in everyday communication is emphasised by activities demonstrating some of the different functions of language.

6   *Patterns in time and space*

Patterns in time and space extends the work of the previous time and space module. It explores the kinds of predictions one can make from understanding patterns and relationships in time and space, like cyclical rhythms, speed and momentum. The later stages of the module broaden the activities beyond physical issues into 'mental' issues. In particular, the module considers how different people come to adopt very different 'mental positions' or view-points. This involves exploring the nature of empathy and prejudice.

7 *Organising and memorising*

Organising and memorising revisits many of the ideas and resources emphasised in previous modules, with an explicit focus on techniques and strategies to facilitate recalling, organising and memorising different types of information. The module emphasises flexible strategic thinking through tasks which prompt pupils to consider which types of organising and memorising techniques and resources should be used for different purposes.

8 *Predicting and deciding*

This final module integrates and sums up aspects from all of the previous modules in the context of a wide range of social, domestic and academic decision-making activities. It highlights the fact that most decision making is based on probabilities rather than certainties. It encourages pupils to consider how different kinds of evidence and information contribute to probabilistic thinking.

The overall modular structure of the course is depicted in Figure 4.7. The diagram illustrates how *Foundations for problem solving* acts as an anchor for the programme by exposing and teaching essential cognitive resources underpinning many aspects of prob-lem solving. The linear nature of the programme is emphasised by the sequenced arrangement of the modules in the 'tree trunk'. Finally, the implications of the work for decision making and problem solving in everyday life is symbolised by the branching foliage.

In summary, the design of each pupil activity is affected by:

1 The modular theme (foundations; analysing and synthesis-ing. . .);
2 The modes of presentation (numerical; tabular; verbal; pictorial. . .);
3 The level of difficulty (amount of information, degree of abstraction and type of operation(s) required);
4 The type of task (stimulus, artificial, naturalistic).

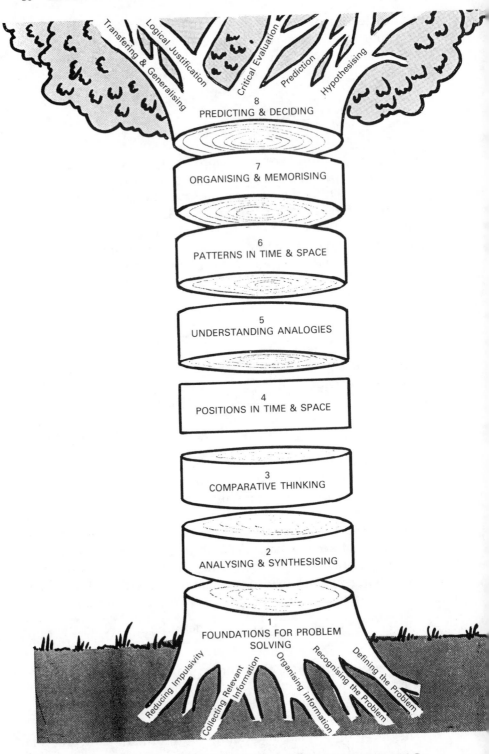

FIGURE 4.7   THE MODULAR STRUCTURE OF STSC

Preparing the ground

A range of considerations need to be thought through before implementing the course. Important amongst these are:

- teacher selection
- teacher training
- teacher support
- pupil selection
- time allocation
- cross-curricular links

Teacher selection

Our own experience suggests that teachers from any phase or specialism can effectively teach the thinking skills course. Nevertheless, there do seem to be a number of prerequisites to success in the classroom. These prerequisites can be usefully considered in the context of Feuerstein's notions of effective mediation. Although some teachers are better mediators than others, there is evidence to suggest that we can learn to become more effective mediators. We will consider the nature of mediation in a later section.

Teacher training

Purchasing the STS Course materials is not conditional on training. With this in mind, we have written the *Handbook* and teacher guidelines with sufficient detail and in a style and format to allow for distanced learning. We appreciate that there will be many teachers already deeply immersed in active learning approaches and problem solving and there will be some who will have experienced training courses in different cognitive skills programmes. These teachers should identify easily with the aims and objectives of STSC and experience minimal difficulty in its classroom implementation.

At the same time there may be many teachers interested in STSC who have experienced very little preparatory training. Undoubtedly, these teachers will need some form of training together with support and guidance. The extent of each will depend on many issues, including the intentions of the user, prior experience, the school context and the pupil target group. Some teachers may like to use the materials as a catalyst or resource to enrich problem-solving activities within their own subject domain. Others may like to use selected modules for particular purposes whilst some teachers may want to teach STSC as an identified subject on the timetable. Naturally, teachers wishing to offer a long-term intensive programme to pupils with special needs will need more guidance and support than the teacher who just wishes to use some of the activities to complement their subject.

Ideally, most teachers will benefit from a one-day awareness session to draw their attention to:

- the aims and purposes of STSC;
- practical issues in using STSC;
- important elements in the *Handbook* and *Teacher guidelines.*

Many teachers will benefit from an additional two-day training course to gain further insight into the organisation and sequencing of the materials as well as 'hands-on contact' and guidance in using the pupil activities.

Teacher support

Cognitive skills work is highly demanding and teachers new to the area will gain enormously from regular meetings to share and discuss ideas with others engaged in similar work. Discussion groups can be even more useful if teachers have the time and opportunity to observe fellow teachers in their own or neighbouring schools. Beyond this, the work can be greatly facilitated by the positive and active interest of members of the senior management team within the school, and/or regular support visits by a trained cognitive skills co-ordinator.

Pupil selection

Although STSC has developed as an outcome of working with 14–16 year old low-achieving adolescents, the materials have been designed for much wider use. During the piloting phase the materials were applied to all ages and ability ranges within secondary education. Furthermore, smaller scale investigations were conducted with top primary children and FE students. In addition, there has been considerable interest from the industrial world, from YTS through to senior management. STSC was cited as an exemplar of good practice in Professor Annette's recent report (1987) to the MSC on *Training in transferable skills*.

Basically the materials have been designed to enable differentiation by outcome. Individuals at different levels of development appear to benefit from the activities by taking the tasks and situations to different levels of reasoning. We do see scope for the materials in many different contexts provided they are properly understood and appropriately used.

At the top primary level the work fits very well with other investigative and problem solving-type activities in addition to linguistic work designed to develop pupils' language functions in the areas of hypothesising, evaluating, justifying opinions and so on.

At the secondary level, the work has been highly successful with mixed ability first year pupils who have greeted the work enthusiastically, seeing it as a natural link between the primary and secondary schools. At a more intensive level the work has been usefully applied to special needs pupils of all ages. Finally, a number of our pilot schools have demonstrated the usefulness of STSC as part of an integrated programme for low-achieving fourth and fifth year pupils.

Within YTS there seems to be a natural link between the cognitive activities in STSC and some of the core competency skills promoted by YTS trainers (especially problem solving and communication skills).

Cross-curricular links

The issues relating to attitudes, beliefs, learning styles and cognitive resources and strategies have wide currency across all subject domains. Under the circumstances, there seems little point in introducing STSC as an isolated course which is separately timetabled without links with other subject areas. As a bare minimum it is important that a group of teachers from different subject disciplines should come together to explore the work and its relationship to their particular specialisms. If the subject is timetabled as a 'thinking skills course' it will be essential for this group of teachers to liaise regularly and find ways of following up thinking skills activities with process work related to their own subject areas. In this way transfer and generalisation is more likely to occur.

Of course this reasoning can be taken a stage further by timetabling the work within the contexts of different subject domains. In our pilot trials with all-ability 11 year olds, one particular school allocated three of its five 50-minute Humanities lessons to STSC on the basis that the issues addressed in STSC were fundamental to Humanities work. It was interesting that the two groups of pupils who received STSC performed much better in the remaining two periods of Humanities than a third group who received their full quota of Humanities lessons.

A second pilot school established cross-curricular links by time-tabling STSC within English, Maths and Environmental Studies. In this particular school pupils gave up one term's Maths, one term's English and one term's Environmental Studies. The three teachers from each of these disciplines were trained in the programme and each taught the course to the same pupils for one term. During the two other terms they each looked for ways of integrating cognitive skills work with their mainstream subject. Teacher fluency with the programme was improved by each of them contributing STSC work to an integrated Life Skills course for older low-achieving pupils.

These are just a few examples of ways in which STSC can be creatively timetabled to facilitate cross-curricular links.

Time allocation

The activities have been structured on the assumption that a minimum of 50 minutes will be allowed for each lesson. Anything less than this will not allow for adequate attention to the introduction, development and summary phases. For younger pupils, we would recommend a minimum of two lessons per week to ensure continuity of ideas between lessons and sufficient practice, familiarity and mastery.

Some special needs pupils with moderate learning difficulties will probably benefit from the whole course and will need a much greater time allocation – probably a minimum of four 50-minute lessons per week. Other special needs pupils with specific learning difficulties might gain from intensive work on particular modules.

There does seem to be a good argument for suggesting that all pupils should be given the opportunity to engage in cognitive skills work as part of their core curriculum with those experiencing particular difficulties receiving more intensive help. As many schools are following a modular curriculum for a significant part of the school week this opens up the possibility of using the early modules as part of a core and reserving some of the later modules, or even parts of them, as short option courses.

However it is timetabled, the impact of STSC with different pupils will be greatly affected by the extent to which teachers actively organise cross-curricular links.

5   The art of effective mediation

In the first few pages of the handbook we referred to Feuerstein's *Mediated Learning Theory*. We have found this aspect of his work extraordinarily useful with respect to classroom practice, and we will now explore this area in greater depth. The choice of the word 'Art' in the title is intentional in the sense that we do not have a precise 'cook book' of the teacher behaviours necessary to bring about cognitive change. Nevertheless, the work of Feuerstein's Israeli team does provide a useful framework within which to consider the role of the teacher.

Feuerstein believes that the human organism is an open system highly malleable and modifiable at all ages and stages of development. The child not only learns from direct experiences – as emphasised by the Stimulus-Organism-Response (S-O-R) Model advocated by Piaget – but, more fundamentally, by experiences filtered and transformed by a mediator (a significant adult) who interposes him or herself between the world of stimuli and the child. Through mediation, critical experiences are emphasised in such a way that the child builds up a cognitive framework in which disparate aspects of experience are meaningfully related. The adult not only intervenes at the stimulus level but also at the response level. For instance, the child is guided by 'Not this way, but that way', or 'Not now, later' and so on. Thus, Feuerstein introduces H into the S-O-R model to represent the significant human who interprets the stimuli to the child, shaping the response and giving meaning behind the activity – changing Piaget's S-O-R Model into S-H-O-H-R.

Feuerstein distinguishes many aspects of mediation, some of which he regards as being culturally determined and others universal. He argues that in order for any interaction to be an example of a mediated learning experience (MLE) three criteria must be satisfied:

1   Intentionality/reciprocity
2   Meaning
3   Transcendence

To mediate effectively the child must understand that the adult has an *intention* to communicate something and the interaction must involve feedback (*reciprocity*) from the child that the adult's intentions are understood. Secondly, the *meaning* and purpose of the interaction must be understood by the child. Finally, the outcomes of the interaction must *transcend* (have consequences and implications far beyond) the immediate needs of the situation. If we consider each of these areas in turn, we can see how they relate to classroom application.

Intentionality/reciprocity

The teacher uses all sorts of explicit and implicit means of establishing pupil attention and conveying intention. Apart from gesture, tone of voice, facial expression and so on, the teacher may use specific techniques to communicate to the pupils commitment, enthusiasm and a powerful intention that something important is to be communicated. In many ways classroom displays, prepared visual aids, exciting starts to lessons and so on all imply teacher intentionality. Before the lesson can proceed the teacher should be picking up clear implicit (body language) and/ or explicit (pupil comments) messages that teacher intentions have been understood.

Meaning

The teacher organises the lesson so that the meaning and significance of the activities are fully understood. This domain overlaps with intentionality in that the teacher's enthusiasm communicates that the activity is important and worthwhile. At the same time, the relevance of the activities needs to be established. For instance, in the early stages of the *Somerset Thinking Skills Course*, it is essential to ensure that the pupils understand what is meant by 'thinking skills' and what might be gained by actively participating in the course. The relevance of the work becomes clearer when pupils can appreciate the transcendent quality, ie the wider significance of many of the activities.

Transcendence

The notion of 'transcendence' is very pertinent to previous discussions on transfer and generalisation and the role of 'metacognition' in fostering this. Pupils need to be helped to understand and articulate important cognitive resources and strategies used in solving particular problems. Moreover, they need help in transferring these cognitive processes to fresh learning situations. Pupils need to appreciate that the main function of working on the tasks in STSC is not to solve those particular problems but to heighten their awareness and control over many cognitive processes that can then be applied spontaneously to many different problems. In other words, they need help in understanding that the work is intending to teach them 'how to learn'.

Competence

Feuerstein also talks about many other important aspects of mediation. Each year he adds more descriptors to embellish and operationalise his ideas. For instance, he refers to the need to mediate for *Competence* which relates to teacher behaviours concerned with developing pupil confidence and self-esteem. This connects with issues such as ensuring an appropriate cognitive match between the learner and the tasks, and the judicious use of encouragement and praise. It is critically important to establish a classroom climate that is free from embarrassment and in which pupils' ideas and viewpoints are listened to and explored. It is also important that unexpected answers or interpretations are carefully considered; even apparent mistakes and mis-interpretations can be invaluable starting points for understanding the kinds of cognitive models the pupils are using in relating to their world. If the teacher closes off discussions by paying relatively little attention to unexpected or incorrect answers, moving on to the next point once the appropriate answer has been given, pupils and teachers will go on missing each other 'in cognitive space'.

Challenge

At the same time, Feuerstein emphasises the importance of mediating for *Challenge*. In our own work we interpret this to mean that children should be given sufficiently difficult tasks to work on. If we always organise learning tasks into easily manageable and neatly sequenced stages, some children may never learn to grapple with complexity. At the same time, if we provide pupils with truly challenging situations we must ensure that they are assisted to recognise the cognitive resources and strategies that will help them manage the task. In other words, pupils need to be helped to learn to simplify complex tasks into manageable chunks that can then be reassembled into meaningful solutions. If the teacher achieves this, both competence and challenge can be effectively mediated. There are many tasks within STSC that look daunting but can be effectively tackled once pupils systematically apply strategic thinking. The teacher needs to know when to stand back and allow the child to succeed alone with great satisfaction and when to intervene to facilitate greater understanding and progress. The principle is 'mediate as little as possible but as much as necessary'.

Sharing behaviour

Another important area for Feuerstein is that of mediating for *Sharing behaviour*. This is a particularly important issue in our work and we have emphasised it in the programme by designing many pupil activities for paired and small group work as well as class discussion.

Individuation and psychological differentiation

There is also the need to mediate for *Individuation and Psychological Differentiation*. In our own programme we have made extensive use of ambiguity and open-ended tasks to foster divergent responses and interpretations, providing the opportunity for many different justifiable viewpoints at varying levels of sophistication. A fuller discussion of Feuerstein's MLE Criteria is given in Blagg, Ballinger and Gardner (1988).

6   A Guide to the teacher guidelines

The guidelines are *not* meant to be *set routines*. They are instead 'small basic meals' that will need elaborating and embellishing according to the types of pupils and the context in which the programme is being used. The activities should be viewed as *springboards* or starting points, with development and generalisation varying according to pupil interests and contributions.

Teachers will note that the guidelines discourage the use of concrete aids, such as templates and measuring devices, in some of the pupil activities. Rules are also introduced on some of the abstract activities preventing pupils from orientating the page in order to make it easier to work out solutions. This is to force pupils to develop strategies enabling mental manipulation of many sources of information simultaneously.

When reading the teacher guidelines it is important to remember that the intended emphasis throughout each of the pupil activities is on developing pupils' own awareness of thinking and problem-solving processes, ie *metacognition*. If pupils can understand and talk about the subtle processes involved in problem solving, it seems likely that they will in time gain control over these processes and transfer them to problem-solving situations beyond school.

Organisation

The teacher guidelines are divided into the following sections:

Description (main features, strategies, resources and key vocabulary)
Introduction

Development
Summary
Transfer and generalisation

We will consider each of these sections in turn.

Description

The description provides the teacher with a general orientation towards the content and nature of each pupil activity. Apart from describing the design and layout of the page, it also refers to explicit and implicit instructions and explains in simple terms how the activity should be interpreted and used.

The description incorporates a number of general aims such as enhancement of self-esteem, improving communication skills and fostering appropriate learning styles (scanning, focusing, reducing impulsivity. . .). This is followed by two sub-sections (*Strategies* and *Resources*) that refer back to the detailed lists provided earlier in this handbook. The pupil activities can be used to expose and develop many different resources and strategies. We have listed some of the key ones, but others may be emphasised in practice according to the way the materials are used and the type of pupils being taught.

Finally, a *Key vocabulary* list includes words that we thought were of particular relevance to the task in hand.

Introduction

The introduction is a 'warming up' period in which the teacher gains the pupils' attention and interest whilst communicating intentionality. This phase of the lesson should also establish the purpose and meaning of the activity. The guidelines provide one or two examples of ways of introducing each activity. Nevertheless, there are endless possibilities for exciting and meaningful introductions, depending on the group involved, the circumstances of the lesson and the interests and enthusiasms of the teacher. We have found the following areas worth considering:

1 It is often helpful to encourage pupils to relate personal experiences that are associated with the intended task page.

This applies particularly to the naturalistic tasks. For instance, in *Foundations for problem solving*, the 'Lost key' activity can be preceded by discussions on objects pupils have lost and the techniques they used in finding them.

2 The use of role play, mime, simulations and games can provide a lively, stimulating and relevant start to a lesson. For example, the 'Living Room' page illustrated earlier (page 36) might be introduced by various activities that heighten pupil awareness of sensory information (mime, blindfold games. . .). Many of the activities in *Positions in time and space* can be introduced with lively games which require precise use of spatial referents.

3 Clever use of provocative open-ended questioning can often stimulate initial discussion and interest. For instance, the 'Chairs' activity in *Analysing and synthesising* might be introduced with a question like, 'What makes a chair a chair?'

4 Wherever possible it is important to vary the introduction format so that the lessons do not become too predictable and routine.

5 It is important that teachers should take every opportunity to create a safe non-critical environment in which even the most reluctant pupils feel able to make a contribution, however small, at the beginning of the lesson.

6 Whilst an exciting and stimulating start to the lesson is important, it is of diminished value if the pupils do not see the connection between this phase of the lesson and the next. Therefore, the introduction should be meaningfully and explicitly related to the development phase.

7 The introduction should *not* extend beyond the first five to ten minutes of the lesson but rather should provide a quick and clear link to the development stage.

Development

During this phase of the lesson the teacher elaborates the meaning of the activity and takes every opportunity to broaden and extend the scope of the work, imbuing it with a purpose and relevance that goes beyond the immediate needs of the task. The intentional use of ambiguity in many of the pupil activities, along with changes in style, format and mode, frequently elicits many conflicting interpretations and definitions of the task and these can be carefully compared and considered. It is important that the teacher gives pupils the opportunity to recognise and define the tasks rather than simply telling them what to do.

In the early stages of this work some teachers and many pupils resent the non-prescriptive nature of the activities. With certain groups the task definition stage can be made less threatening by organising it as a group activity. Furthermore, pupils can learn to enjoy this part of the lesson, particularly when they realise that their point of view is just as valid as the very different opinions of others in the class.

The teacher's job involves helping the pupils to explain their interpretations with reference to the evidence and prompting them to consider the basis of their assumptions. Frequently, it is necessary to establish a consensus view of the task requirements before encouraging pupils to *consider possible strategies, anticipate problems, compare* with previous activities and ultimately *develop a plan.*

On many occasions we have suggested that the planning and execution phases of the tasks should be organised as paired or small group activities. There are various ways in which this can be achieved and we talk about managing group work and discussions in a later section.

The STSC materials can be used very flexibly with group and class discussion work following up many different avenues. Practical experience with the programme has demonstrated that it is all too easy to run out of time at the end of the lesson so that there is no opportunity for the summary or transfer and generalisation phases. If this happens regularly, much of the value of the programme will be undermined. Accordingly, it is essential that teachers keep a careful check on the timing and pacing of the lesson so that 20 minutes are allowed for these final phases.

Summary

The summary phase gives the pupils the opportunity to review the nature and purpose of the activity and the kinds of skills and vocabulary they have learnt in the process. The teacher's role in this will be to ask, 'What have you learnt during this activity?' helping pupils, where necessary, to attend to important features of the activity and articulate the relevant process issues.

Transfer and generalisation

Fostering transfer and generalisation is the very basis of STSC. These issues overlap with Feuerstein's notion of 'transcendence'. All STSC activities are designed to enable the teacher to mediate for transcendence in the sense that the purpose of each activity goes far beyond the immediate demands of the task. We are not so much concerned with children becoming better at solving the STSC problems. We are more concerned that they learn to use the tasks and situations to acquire and gain control over new skills and strategies, so that they can deploy them flexibly in novel situations.

In view of these considerations, attention to this area is the most crucial part of any lesson ending. For these reasons we have included this as a separate section in the teacher guidelines. Teachers will note that the section focuses largely on suggestions for stimulating the pupils to think about where the skills and strategies learnt in STSC apply to other situations in their school and everyday life. However, before we consider this area more fully, mention must be made of the importance of attending to transfer and generalisation throughout each phase of every lesson.

Each new activity provides an opportunity for the teacher to assess and encourage transfer of ideas *within* the programme. Pupil activities have been grouped and sequenced with this in mind. Each module addresses a particular theme with activities requiring similar strategies and resources. The early activities in each module introduce a number of strategies and resources important to the theme and these are then practised through closely related tasks, to establish confidence and fluency. Gradually, pupil activities are made more difficult by some or all of the following:

- increasing the amounts of information involved;
- increasing the range of modes used;
- making the tasks more abstract;
- changing the style and content.

Thus, strategies and resources acquired earlier are elaborated and practised in progressively more difficult and dissimilar tasks to those originally introduced. Increasingly, pupils are expected to break down new tasks into manageable steps that are closely related to the previous simpler activities. If pupils do not make spontaneous comparisons teachers will need to prompt with questions like,

What is similar about this activity to previous ones?
What is different?
Have you learnt anything previously that will help you with this task?

This should increase pupils' awareness of previously acquired skills. If pupils still cannot make the necessary connections, teachers may need to draw their attention to similar activities previously encountered and to assist the pupils in drawing up a list of similarities and differences. Once the task has been simplified into manageable steps the pupils may need assistance in integrating the various aspects of the task.

Whilst the transfer of ideas within the programme is important, the transfer of ideas to fresh contexts *beyond* the programme is the main aim. When pupils can learn to apply skills and strategies to very different situations beyond the programme we refer to this as 'generalisation'. Many pupils do not find this easy, particularly in the early stages of the course, and teachers will need to come well prepared with plenty of examples that make the links between the course and reality clear to the pupils. As the pupils gain confidence and become more aware of their own problem-solving techniques, they should begin to transfer skills spontaneously to new tasks within the programme and to generalise spontaneously to fresh contexts outside the programme.

We have tried to help pupils and teachers in this process by using a range of task types. Some are very remote from real life experiences (the abstract artificial tasks) and some are quite closely related to familiar everyday problems (naturalistic tasks). For both task types we include a few examples of practical situations that require the deployment of similar strategies alongside suggestions for further discussion. Of course there are many more possibilities and teachers may find it useful to compile their own list of ideas that have proved successful. Finally, a third type of task (stimulus) which occurs regularly throughout each module has been specifically designed for discussion work to provoke connections between ideas, strategies and principles across many different areas. Whilst we do not expect every child to be able to transfer and generalise ideas from every STSC task page, we do hope that the inclusion of many different scenarios and task types will enable many more children to make the kinds of connections and links with reality that we are looking for.

Promoting the transfer and generalisation of skills should not be left to the 'thinking skills teacher' but should be the shared responsibility of all staff. However, this can only be achieved through INSET and discussion groups set up to foster cross-curricular links and staff awareness of the aims and purpose of STSC. We have made reference to specific curriculum links at various points in the course as well as making suggestions for follow-up projects.

At a more sophisticated level, generalisation is fostered through processes of *induction* and *deduction*. The many different tasks and contexts used within each theme enable general rules and principles to be established through a process of induction. For instance, pupils might learn from a number of different modular activities that precision and accuracy in labelling is generally helpful in organising the visually confusing tasks. Pupils might then deduce that principles such as this are widely applicable to many everyday confusing situations. Indeed, such notions can be tried and tested.

At key points within each module 'mastery' tasks are introduced to check for previous learning and the extent of transfer and generalisation.

7 Classroom organisation and management

Lesson preparation

It is important to appreciate that each pupil activity is part of a sequence. Therefore, rather than prepare one activity at a time, it is helpful if teachers think through a unit of activity pages to appreciate the sequence and structure involved. Attention to the following areas is essential:

1 Always complete the activity in full before attempting to use it in the classroom.
2 Note any key features, implicit and explicit instructions, paying particular attention to ambiguity and complexity.
3 Note the vocabulary that must be introduced to equip pupils with the verbal tools necessary to complete the task.
4 Analyse the kinds of strategies and resources that pupils will need to deploy.
5 Anticipate possible difficulties that pupils may encounter in working on the activity, bearing in mind the task content, mode, complexity. . . considering strategies to overcome or remedy anticipated problems.
6 Think in terms of overcoming difficulties at any of the three phase levels of mental activity, ie gathering the information, thinking it through and responding.
7 Plan a novel, exciting and meaningful start to each lesson and prepare practical examples and activities for transfer and generalisation.
8 Consider how the activity can be best organised in terms of independent, paired, small group or class work.
9 Be realistic about the time allocation required for each phase of the lesson. Do not attempt to overload any of the stages by attending to too many issues. There are always plenty of

opportunities to return to important points throughout the programme.

10 Keep a record of general problems faced by the class and particular problems encountered by individual pupils so that these can be followed up in later lessons.

Practical arrangements

There are a number of issues worth considering, including:

- creating a comfortable classroom environment;
- seating arrangements;
- visual aids.

Creating a comfortable classroom environment

A comfortable classroom environment communicates teacher enthusiasm and intentionality – important prerequisites for any lesson. A key area for consideration involves the display of attractively mounted examples of pupils' work. This can greatly encourage pupil effort, provide a sense of ownership in the room and offer a model of the orderly presentation of ideas. The use of plants and other 'homely touches' can make the classroom more welcoming. Finally, it is important to ensure that essential equipment like pencils, rubbers, rough paper and dictionaries is readily to hand, and that there is appropriate storage space for pupil files of work.

Seating arrangements

In most STSC classes teachers need to be able to move smoothly between class discussions, small group, paired and independent working. For class discussions, the ideal seating arrangement is a 'U' shape so that all of the pupils have eye contact with each other and with the teacher. The teacher can maintain a prominent position in the open part of the 'U', move about behind the pupils or sit with the pupils as part of the 'U'.

The 'U' shape is also fine for independent and/or paired working. However, it does mean that pupils will need to rearrange their chairs for group work. Furthermore, the 'U' shape loses its advantage with larger numbers of pupils as the 'U' has to be so extended. For these reasons some teachers may find it more useful to arrange the pupils in small groups. This is ideal for group work, paired and/or independent working but not so useful for class discussion work.

Finally, it can be very useful to have an easy means of bringing the whole class together as a small, tight unit from time to time. This formation can be useful for giving instructions or demonstrations or even for general discussion purposes.

A few teachers are fortunate in having at their disposal large rooms, with ready organised facilities for each of these arrangements. More commonly however, physical constraints often militate against the ideal and compromise arrangements are necessary. Under these conditions it is essential that teachers think carefully about the best possible compromise.

Visual aids

The use of an overhead projector is strongly advised for a number of reasons:

1 It enables the teacher to use pre-prepared diagrams, notes and stimulus materials that are easily transportable and re-usable.
2 There are many times when it is useful to discuss features of the task activity without issuing the page to the pupils. This can be very helpful in preventing the pupils from impulsively working on the task before they have recognised and defined the problem. An OHP transparency can be made of each task page to allow for this.
3 The OHP allows the teacher to make notes during discussions without losing eye contact with the class.
4 Elected scribes from each small group can be given OHP transparencies to record their findings and methods of work. Spokespersons from each small group can then use the OHT notes as aide-memoires in reporting back to the class as a whole.
5 Areas of difficulty and ambiguity can be worked through on the OHT task pages – by the teacher or by a class volunteer – with everybody having a clear view of procedure.

Managing discussions

The notion of discussion conveys different meanings to different teachers. Some use the term to refer to occasions when the children are assembled as a class with the teacher asking many questions. The fact that pupils do not initiate any questions or exchange ideas with one another does not seem to be a concern. It has been suggested that a 'good' discussion involves many pupils heatedly expressing their opinions. However, whether they listen to one another or establish any common agreement on an issue or a problem is frequently not considered. In the context of STSC, we would not regard either of these scenarios as exemplars of good discussion work. We would suggest that good discussion work is a rare commodity in many classrooms. It is far more typical for the teacher to engage in closed question and answer sessions where the teacher initiates the questions and the interaction is completed as soon as the 'correct' answer is supplied. All too often, unusual or alternative responses that are not anticipated by the teacher are overlooked, consciously ignored or, worse still, dismissed without consideration.

It is important to distinguish between guided and open-ended discussions. In a guided discussion, the teacher occupies a central position, directing and leading the group. There will be a strong emphasis on statements and questions which clarify and summarise issues and the group will frequently be refocused on the main aspects of the activity. Typically, the teacher will have a very clear plan of what is to be gained from the discussion and at least general notions about the kinds of replies expected to questions posed. In contrast, open-ended discussions involve the teacher in very little leading and directing. Frequently questions for which there are many different answers are intentionally posed. The teacher may have a general plan and intention in setting up the discussion but will be very ready to follow up pupil interests, enthusiasms and ideas, even if they are not directly related to the teacher's prior notions. In STSC we advocate that teachers should engage in both guided and open-ended discussions. However, even in open-ended discussions the teacher will have a hidden agenda and will always be conscious of the metacognitive aspects of the lesson. The course aims to foster independent, autonomous learning and as such the teacher will want to prompt and lead the discussion as little as possible but as much as necessary. The style of discussion will also be regulated to some degree by the phase of the lesson and the type of task involved. For instance, the stimulus tasks lend themselves to more open-ended discussion work whereas the abstract tasks are likely to require a more guided discussion. In either case the introductory phases of lessons will tend to encourage a more open-ended approach whereas the summary phase is likely to be more guided.

There are a number of general principles and considerations that apply to all types of discussion work. We can consider these under the following headings:

- Teacher role
- Asking questions
- Teacher response
- Standards of conduct
- Pupil roles
- Overcoming problems
- Small group work

Teacher role

Perhaps we should have referred to 'teacher roles' rather than 'role'. In any discussion, the teacher needs to perform a delicate balancing act, knowing when to enforce procedural authority, when to act as a neutral chairperson and when to step back and allow the pupils to conduct their own discussion without interference or guidance.

In the guidelines we have intended to imply that the teacher should not be viewed by the pupils as the source of all knowledge and wisdom but rather as someone who shares in and facilitates discussion. The teacher models exploratory and questioning behaviour in the search for clarification and resolution of problems. In this situation, the teacher no longer occupies the centre stage with respect to 'knowing' but is rather an equal participant in the problem-solving process. Often the teacher will physically demonstrate this role by sitting with the pupils in the 'U' shape while a pupil volunteer occupies a more central position, for example when justifying a viewpoint with reference to notes or a diagram on the OHP. On other occasions, when the pupils are discussing ideas amongst themselves in a mature way, the teacher may take up a position at the back of the room outside the 'U' shape. On the other hand, if the discussion is too slow or ragged, the teacher may need to take up a more central position, refocusing the group and prompting involvement through carefully chosen comments and questions.

Asking questions

Successful discussion work should involve the pupils as well as the teacher in initiating questions. Pupils should be challenging and questioning other pupils and, if appropriate, the teacher. If the teacher is the sole initiator of questions, it is unlikely that true discussion is occurring.

We have designed many of the STSC activities as paired or small group tasks that are specifically directed towards 'learning to ask the right kinds of questions' to obtain particular types of information. In the final phase of each lesson, when pupil solutions and methods of working are being compared, justified and evaluated as a class, teachers can actively encourage pupils to question and challenge each other by prompting with remarks like, 'If you don't understand what John is saying, ask some questions to help him clarify his explanation.'

Naturally, there will be times when the teacher does take the lead role in questioning. This occurs especially in the early stages of the course and at times during the lesson when the teacher is trying to initiate a discussion. In these instances, the teacher uses questioning to raise ambiguities, stimulate interest and provoke thought. Some pupils may feel self-conscious and vulnerable and be reluctant to participate whilst others may dominate with enthusiastic and sometimes impulsive contributions.

It can be very helpful to the more reticent pupils if everyone is obliged to make a contribution, however small, in the very early stages of the lesson. This can often break the ice, enabling pupils to risk participation in the future. A safe way of doing this involves asking a very simple straightforward question related to the topic in hand that everybody can make a comment on. 'Name one type of feeling or emotion,' might be useful as a starter question in one of the *Comparative thinking* activities. Pupils may be asked to contribute one suggestion in turn. However, greater involvement can be achieved by allowing the first pupil to contribute to choose the next person, and so on. In this way the pupils have more active control over events and are more likely to remain alert as they are not sure when they will be chosen. Children who hesitate can be given extra time to think, with the teacher returning to them after the rest of the pupils have contributed.

It is useful to think in terms of 'open' and 'closed' questions. We refer to a question as being 'closed' if it requires a 'yes' or 'no' answer or one particular factual answer. The following are examples of closed questions:

Did you develop a plan?
Did you check your work?
What are the names of the five senses?
What do the instructions say?
Where do we record our answers?

In contrast, open questions offer many more possibilities for pupils to contribute their own ideas and viewpoints. They do not require a short 'yes' or 'no' response and the teacher is not looking for one specific answer. Open questions are often asking for opinions and/or explanations. For instance:

How did you develop a plan?
How do you know that's the right answer?
What do you think the problem is?
Why do you say that?
Where else does this happen in life?

Open questions offer pupils greater scope but still do not guarantee their involvement and participation. This raises the important issue of how teachers respond to pupil contributions.

Teacher responses

Many pupils do not participate because they are not given sufficient time to think. It is essential that teachers learn to wait for contributions, even if this involves a period of silence.

Whilst it is important to encourage pupils to put forward ideas, effusive and selective use of praise can give the impression that some ideas are better than others. It may be appropriate to convey this impression at the evaluation stage, but not during the early parts of the lesson when the teacher should be encouraging maximum participation and the sharing of many alternative interpretations, definitions and viewpoints. In general, it is safer to use 'low key' and non-judgmental responses to pupil contributions, such as 'That's interesting.' 'Yes, that's one way of looking at it.' 'Mmmm.' In many cases, the teacher can communicate interest and recognition through gesture, facial expression and eye contact without saying anything. Simply listening to and considering pupil ideas is the best way of validating and encouraging contributions.

Very often teachers want to explore pupil ideas further, to check the meaning of a particular communication. In this situation, a positive comment like, 'That's interesting,' preceding, 'Say more about that,' is likely to provide the pupil with the necessary encouragement and confidence to expand on a viewpoint.

Standards of conduct

Managing guided or even open-ended discussions does not imply that the teacher should surrender authority. Class discussion cannot proceed if there is a total 'free for all'. The extent to which the teacher needs to intervene and remind pupils of rules and codes of acceptable conduct will depend on the age and maturity of the pupils and the prior relationships that exist between them and the teacher. As a bare minimum, the following rules should be established at the outset:

1   Only one person should speak at any one time.
2   Everybody else listens whilst one person is speaking.
3   All contributions are entertained even if they do not precisely fit the topic or expectations.
4   Any questions or challenges are expressed in clear and polite terms.
5   Any critical feedback is directed at comments and not at the pupils who made them.

Pupil roles

In both class and small group discussion work, teachers should be mindful of the specialised pupil roles that are likely to develop. Indeed, the teacher may need to cultivate these distinct roles to maximise the benefits of sharing behaviour and to encourage particular pupils to take on certain responsibilities. For instance, pupils might be encouraged in playing the role of:

1 Proposer of ideas
2 Active supporter of another pupil's ideas
3 Challenger of ideas
4 Seeker of precise and accurate information (provoking other pupils to explain, clarify and justify their ideas)
5 Information giver and dictionary consultant
6 Summariser (collating all responses submitted by the group/class)
7 Scribe (using the board/OHP)
8 Timekeeper

Overcoming problems

It is common for pupils to be over-dependent on the teacher, feeling unable to contribute unless invited to do so. The 'U' shape furniture configuration can help here by removing the teacher from a prominent position and giving eye-contact between pupils. Encouraging pupils to question one another can also be helpful, eg 'Does anyone want to ask Lawrence about his answer?' It is important to avoid consistent eye-contact with the speaker. Pupils should be encouraged to address the class rather than the teacher.

Dominant pupils can be referred to in order to encourage other pupils to contribute, eg 'What does anyone else think of Lawrence's idea?'. More reticent pupils can be encouraged to enlarge on their brief statements, eg 'That's interesting, say more'.

Sometimes a clique of pupils will opt out and form an 'out group'. This can be tackled by asking members of the 'out group' to make contributions and/or by splitting the group into sub-groups, giving opportunities for the quieter ones to talk.

Socially isolated pupils can be helped by ensuring that they are not ridiculed by other, more outgoing pupils and by carefully choosing more sympathetic partners for paired and small group working. It is important to bear in mind that the silent pupil may be participating through listening!

Jokers, disrupters and other attention seekers should not be unwittingly rewarded for their behaviour by constant rebukes. It is better to contrive situations where the child can be praised for appropriate behaviour. It is also useful to consciously give recognition to a pupil sitting near the 'joker' who is modelling more appropriate behaviour. Attention can be turned to the 'joker' when he or she resumes more acceptable behaviour. Finally, it can be helpful to treat all contributions to discussions seriously so that extroverts get merit only for their ideas and not for their silly performance.

Sometimes two extreme positions may occur in a class discussion resulting in arguments, with each side making little attempt to understand the other point of view. In this instance, pupils' attention should be focused on analysing the logical basis for their different viewpoints and if necessary make explicit the kinds of assumptions they are holding and evidence for these. Occasionally, with more immature groups, it is a good idea to introduce some neutral material as a 'cooling off' task encouraging reflection.

On other occasions the class may be united in one point of view and unable to consider alternatives. Here, it is important for the teacher to provoke disagreement and disequilibrium, 'throwing a spanner in the works' to provoke divergent responses. This can be achieved by providing examples of situations that run counter to pupils' viewpoint or even by asking whether pupils can think of any situations where their views would not be upheld.

Small group work

> If we want (pupils) to understand what we teach, we must give them the opportunity to personalise knowledge. We cannot give (pupils) knowledge; we can only help them to come to know.
>
> (Reid, Forrestal and Cook, 1982)

Reid et al have published a very helpful book on small group work in the classroom, arising out of the *Language and learning project*. Many of the activities in STSC lend themselves to small group work. We feel that this provides a good opportunity for pupils to develop their own understanding of problem-solving situations; sharing, comparing and evaluating ideas and learning to appreciate each others' strengths and abilities in different roles. Small group work also provides an ideal context for enhancing pupils' oracy skills. This area has been the subject of considerable interest in Wiltshire (Wiltshire Oracy Project) and recently the Schools Curriculum Development Council has established a National Oracy Project.

The teacher guidelines for each pupil activity offer suggestions on ways of organising small group work. Ideally, most STSC lessons should involve a carefully considered balance of class, group, paired and independent working.

Derivations

The use of precise and accurate language is essential to problem solving, and is strongly emphasised throughout STSC. A useful way of exploring and extending pupils' understanding of new words is to look at their Greek and Latin derivations. This often leads to a stimulating discussion of meaning, ranging far beyond the needs of the particular STSC activity being tackled.

8   Diagnostic use of STSC materials

The *Somerset Thinking Skills Course* has been designed to teach, discuss and generalise specific concepts, skills and strategies involved in problem solving. In so doing, different pupil activities expose the need for, and offer the chance to assess, pupil ability to handle these processes. Earlier in this manual we referred to Feuerstein's Cognitive Map. Each activity in STSC can be analysed according to the parameters of this map to determine the specific area or areas of a task that hinder an individual's learning.

In mediating with individual pupils during the development phase of the lesson the teacher should become aware of the particular stumbling blocks holding up the child's ability to tackle the problem. Careful analysis of the child's methods of work should reveal the precise dimension of the Map in which the problem lies. Teachers need to appreciate that problems may occur in a number of areas:

Content

Some pupils may be unable to tackle the task simply because the subject matter is unfamiliar to them. In this instance the teacher must make sure that all the pupils have the basic knowledge prerequisite to doing the task. The fact that some children do not possess the knowledge on which the task is based should not handicap them in being able to work on the activity.

Mode

Frequently it is the mode of presentation that acts as a problem for many children. A pupil may cope well with a pictorial presentation but have difficulty in handling a similar task depicted in verbal, tabular or even diagrammatic format. STSC compensates for this by providing similar activities in a wide range of modes offering the teacher the opportunity to assess and mediate for any particular difficulties.

Operations

This term is used to refer to the mental structure through which information is processed, ranging from the business of simple recognition through to the use of analogies. In this aspect of Feuerstein's work there is considerable overlap with Piaget's ideas. Feuerstein argues that high-level operational thinking is based on a series of lower-level fundamental processes which are open to change with the right kind of mediated experiences. Many of the tasks in STSC are quite sophisticated (eg understanding analogies). However, we have made every attempt to guide the teacher and pupil towards the manageable component processes involved in the more sophisticated operations.

Phase

Phase is a somewhat artificial way of breaking down a mental act into three broad areas – *input, elaboration* and *output*. Undoubtedly, there are children who experience major problems with one particular phase. However, in analysing this area it is easy to oversimplify and thereby focus on inappropriate aspects of the individual's difficulties. For instance, the impulsive child often has difficulty in selecting appropriate information but is frequently treated as though the problem is at the elaboration and/or output stages.

Many of the issues referred to in the STSC cognitive resources and cognitive strategy lists can be grouped into the three phases of the mental act. For instance, handling several sources of information at once may be a problem at the input, elaboration and output phases. Using a systematic search technique to ensure that all relevant information has been gathered can be considered as part of the input phase; clarity of expression in describing a viewpoint would fit the output phase.

Complexity

Many pupils have problems because of the level of difficulty presented in the activity. This may be due to the sheer quantity of information and the amount of detail that needs to be handled simultaneously while working on the task. In this case, teachers need to encourage pupils to recognise a major principle of STSC

– that complex tasks can be handled successfully by breaking the information down into smaller, manageable units.

Abstraction

As the mental act moves further and further away from the concrete events on which it operates, the more abstract it becomes. Ultimately, abstract thinking would involve purely hypothetical propositions. In some instances, pupils can cope with quite sophisticated and complex tasks that are still embedded in concrete examples but experience enormous problems once they become removed from reality and encoded in symbolism. Tasks in STSC are sequenced to move through stimulus, artificial and naturalistic types of activities. The degree of abstraction in each type of task gradually increases within each module and as the pupils move through the course. The progression is not linear as we regularly refer back to more concrete situations. In general the artificial tasks tend to be abstract.

Efficiency

The level of efficiency concerns the speed and accuracy of the mental act at the input, elaboration and output stages. It is a function of all of the other dimensions on the cognitive map, but is also influenced by factors like anxiety and motivation. The notion of efficiency emphasises the importance of allowing children time to think. Many children can perform complex, sophisticated operations if given sufficient time. The STSC materials are designed to encourage and develop precision, accuracy and reflective thinking. At the same time, teachers should be aware of the need to encourage pupils to appreciate that efficiency involves both accuracy and speed. In addition, considering efficiency does involve pupils in being able to select and adapt relevant strategies rather than keeping to one familiar, safe but long-winded algorithm.

Evaluating the lesson

We can consider evaluation from the point of view of both teacher and pupil.

Pupil evaluation

The importance of pupils evaluating methods of work and what they have learnt has already been emphasised in the *Summary* and *Transfer and generalisation* section of the teacher guidelines. We are including it again as a separate issue because we feel that there is merit in using some 'formal' kind of evaluation system to prompt pupils to reflect on their own progress and encourage both teacher and pupil efforts.

Teachers are advised to design their own pupil checklists to suit their particular classes. Ideally, different styles of checklist should be designed, emphasising various aspects of the work, to prompt pupils to think about their own thinking. We would suggest that checklists are best used on a fortnightly or monthly basis after a series of activities, enabling both the teacher and the pupils to reflect on progress. There is little point in attempting to rush through some kind of 'tick system' at the end of every lesson as this is not likely to achieve the desired ends.

Figures 8.1 and 8.2 show examples of checklists that pupils can complete in discussion with a partner.

Teacher evaluation

Teacher evaluation implies two things. First, there is the teacher's on-going record keeping and notes about each pupil's progress. Second, there is the teacher's regular self appraisal of his or her own classroom behaviour and management with respect to achieving the goals of the programme.

With respect to the first of these two areas, most teachers will have their own well-established record-keeping systems. Some will like to keep a diary of events, noting any 'critical incidents' implying a fundamental change in the behaviour of the group or one or more of the pupils. Others may prefer to keep a profile of each pupil in the class, noting significant changes in key areas at regular intervals. With regard to critical changes directly related to the programme the teacher will find it helpful to refer to many different issues including those noted in the sample checklist (taken from Blagg 1988) shown in Figure 8.3. If the programme is being used with children with learning and behavioural difficulties the class teacher may expect to see an improvement in pupils' self-esteem and more regular school attendance.

FIGURE 8.1   STSC PUPIL QUESTIONNAIRE

NAME ....   MODULE ....

Discuss the following questions with a partner and give yourself a score by ringing the appropriate statement in each case.

		1	2	3	4
ATTITUDE	How did I approach the task?	with no interest	with some interest	positively	enthusiastically
CONFIDENCE	Was I confidence in tackling the task?	very unsure of myself	unsure of myself	confident	very confident
STYLE	How much time did I take to stop and think?	none at all	not enough	sufficient	a great deal
RECOGNISING	Did I find the main problem?	with great difficulty	with some difficulty	easily	very easily
DEFINING	Did I describe the main problem?	with great difficulty	with some difficulty	easily	very easily
PLANNING	Did I develop a useful plan?	inadequately	needed improvement	adequately	very successfully
MONITORING	Did I monitor my progress as I worked	not at all	rarely	occasionally	frequently
	Did I change my approach?	never	sometimes	often	always
EVALUATING	Did I do well?	with great difficulty	with some difficulty	easily	very easily
	Did I understand why I succeeded or had difficulties?	not at all	a little	to a large extent	fully
COMMUNICATING	Did I explain my ideas and approach clearly to others?	not at all	a little	to a large extent	fully
SKILLS AND KNOWLEDGE	How many new words, ideas or thinking skills did I learn?	none	a few	some	many
TRANSFERRING	How much did I learn that could help me with a similar problem?	nothing at all	very little	quite a lot	a great deal
GENERALISING	How much did I learn that could help me with any problem?	nothing at all	very little	quite a lot	a great deal

What are my areas of strength? ———————————————————————————

What are my areas of weakness? ———————————————————————————

How can I make improvements? ———————————————————————————

FIGURE 8.2   PUPIL CHECKLIST

Name .... Module ....

Work in pairs. Discuss and agree which thinking skills and strategies you have used in this lesson

Thinking Skills	Dates				
Labelling					
Describing					
Comparing					
Classifying					
Analysing					
Synthesizing					
Searching Systematically					
Scanning					
Selecting relevant Information					
Recognising implicit cues					
Reading explicit Instructions					
Brainstorming					
Hypothesising					
Anticipating					
Predicting					
Planning					
Mentally visualising					
Eliminating					
Counting					
Checking					
Summarising					
Revising					
Evaluating					
Communicating clearly					
Explaining					
Justifying					

FIGURE 8.3 · TEACHER OBSERVATION SCHEDULE

School ....   Pupil's Name..

Name of Teacher...   Year Group ....

Subject ....   Date..

The following pairs of statements describe aspects of the child's behaviour in the classroom. Using your observations of the child tick the appropriate number according to the following guide:

1   The left hand statement always applies.
2   The left hand statement sometimes applies.
3   The left and right hand statements apply equally.
4   The right hand statement sometimes applies.
5   The right hand statement always applies.

TYPICALLY THIS PUPIL:

1 Is self-disciplined in class.	1	2	3	4	5	Is disruptive in class.
2 Settles down to work quickly.	1	2	3	4	5	Takes a long time to settle down to work.
3 Concentrates right up to the end of the lesson.	1	2	3	4	5	Tends to become unsettled towards the end of the lesson.
4 Is highly responsive to direct questioning.	1	2	3	4	5	Is unresponsive to direct questioning, i.e. remains silent and sullen.
5 Actively contributes to class discussion work.	1	2	3	4	5	Switches off during class discussion.
6 Is self-motivated towards classwork.	1	2	3	4	5	Is unmotivated towards classwork.
7 Asks for help when in difficulty.	1	2	3	4	5	Never asks for help when in difficulty.
8 Produces neat, carefully organised work.	1	2	3	4	5	Produces untidy slapdash work.
9 Strives towards precision and accuracy.	1	2	3	4	5	Does not appreciate the relevance of precision and accuracy.
10 Usually gives relevant and complete answers to questions.	1	2	3	4	5	Frequently supplies irrelevant or incomplete replies to questions.
11 Willingly helps other pupils in the class.	1	2	3	4	5	Shows no evidence of concern for other pupils.
12 Listens to other pupils' comments during discussions.	1	2	3	4	5	Never listens to other pupils' comments during discussions.
13 Will defend own opinions on the basis of logical evidence.	1	2	3	4	5	Fails to supply logical evidence to support opinions.
14 Can describe to others a number of different strategies for solving a problem.	1	2	3	4	5	Is unable to describe more than one way of solving a particular problem.
15 Shows evidence of using precise problem solving vocabulary.	1	2	3	4	5	Shows no evidence of using precise problem solving vocabulary.
16 Arrives at lessons on time.	1	2	3	4	5	Is frequently late for lessons.
17 Arrives with appropriate equipment.	1	2	3	4	5	Never arrives with appropriate equipment.

18	Produces work with relatively few errors.	1	2	3	4	5	Produces work showing frequent errors and erasures.
19	Takes responsibility for catching-up on work missed.	1	2	3	4	5	Never spontaneously bothers to make-up for missed work.
20	Spontaneously reads and follows instructions carefully before starting on a task.	1	2	3	4	5	Is constantly making mistakes because of failing to consider all of the instructions carefully beforehand.
21	Shows evidence of being able to handle two or more sources of information at one time when solving problems.	1	2	3	4	5	Approaches problems using a random trial and error strategy or only one source of information/ dimension at one time.
22	Readily completes homework assignments.	1	2	3	4	5	Rarely manages to complete homework.
23	Approaches new tasks and work with confidence.	1	2	3	4	5	Tends to be apprehensive about unfamiliar tasks and new work.
24	Spontaneously makes links across different curricular areas.	1	2	3	4	5	Has difficulty in making links between curricular areas.
25	*Uses a dictionary spontaneously.	1	2	3	4	5	Actively avoids dictionary work.

* Please complete only if pupil has a dictionary available in class.

With regard to the second area of teacher evaluation it is important that teachers should reflect on their role in organising the lesson and mediating to the pupils. It can be useful to review the extent to which important cognitive resources have been mediated. A simple checklist like the one shown in Figure 8.4 can act as an *aide mémoire* of important issues. Finally, teachers should consider the extent to which they are mediating for intentionality/reciprocity, meaning and transcedence. A detailed consideration of these issues is given in Blagg, Ballinger and Gardner (1988).

FIGURE 8.4   COGNITIVE RESOURCES TEACHER CHECKLIST

A   Does the teacher organise the lesson and mediate in such a way that pupils appreciate the need:-

1   *to attend to detail* systematically in gathering information, defining the problem and responding to the problem

2   *for precision and accuracy* in gathering information, defining the problem and responding to the task

3   *to label precisely and use appropriate vocabulary* in working on the task pages. Key vocabulary is carefully defined with reference to a dictionary where appropriate

4   *for speed and efficiency* in all aspects of problem solving, i.e. speed is encouraged without jeopardising precision and accuracy

5   *to recognise and define the problem*

6   *to distinguish between relevant and irrelevant* details

7   *to make comparisons* between the task in hand and previous expriences that have required similar processes

8   *to organise, group, categorise and classify* where appropriate so that more complex information can be handled

9   *to anticipate and plan* for difficulties. Pupils are helped to hypothesise about the outcome if certain courses of action are taken

10   *to evaluate and justify their hypotheses and viewpoints* by reference to appropriate evidence, cues and clues

11   *to extract rules and principles* from the task in hand to apply to wider situations

12   *for summarising* what they have learnt.

B   Does the teacher differentiate between able pupils and those with specific learning difficulties, by:
   • *helping those with problems in specific modes of presentation,* (ie verbal, numerical, figural, diagrammatic, tabular, pictorial, cartoon);

C   Does the teacher *establish a safe, embarrassment-free climate* in which those pupils with a lack of confidence or reluctance to participate, may be willing to risk involvement.

References

Annett, J. (1987) *Training in transferable skills.* Final report on a project sponsored by the Manpower Services Commission

Blagg, N.R. (1984) *Introduction of Feuerstein's Instrumental Enrichment Programme into four Bridgwater Secondary Schools – An Evaluation Framework,* Somerset County Council

—— (1988) *The Somerset Evaluation of Feuerstein's Instrumental Enrichment Programme. An exploration of pupil and teacher change* (in preparation)

Blagg, N.R., Ballinger, M.P., Gardner, R.J. (1988) *Developing Cognitive Skills – Feuerstein's Ideas Reappraised* Routledge and Kegan Paul (in preparation)

Brown, A.L. (1974) 'The Role of Strategic Behaviour in Retardate Memory' in N.R. Ellis (ed) *International Review and Research in Mental Retardation,* New York, Academic Press

Campione, J.C., Brown, A.L., Ferrara, R.A. (1982) 'Mental retardation and intelligence' in R.J. Sternberg (ed) *Handbook of human intelligence* Cambridge University Press

Chipman, S.F., Segal, J.W. and Glaser, R. (1985) *Thinking and Learning Skills,* Volume 2, 'Research and Open Questions Hillsdale New Jersey: Lawrence Erlbaum

Clarke, A.D.B. and Clarke, A.M. (1976) *Early experience: myth and evidence* New York: Free Press

de Bono, E (1973) *CoRT Thinking,* Blandford, Dorset, England. Direct Education Services Ltd

Downs, S and Perry, P. (1984) *Developing Skilled Learners: Learning to Learn in YTS.* MSC R & D Rep. 22

Feuerstein, R., Rand, Y. and Hoffman, M.B. (1979) *The Dynamic Assessment of Retarded Performers* Baltimore, University Park Press

—— (1980) *Instrumental Enrichment* Baltimore, University Park Press

Flavell, J.H. (1976) 'Metacognitive aspects of problem-solving' In L.B. Resnick (ed) *The Nature of Intelligence* Hillsdale, New Jersey: Erlbaum

Kagan, J., Rosman, B.L., Day, D., Albert, J., and Phillips, W. (1964) *Information Processing in the Child: Significance of Analytic and Reflective Attitudes.* Psychological Monographs, 78. (Whole No. 578).

Lawrence, D. (1988) *Enhancing Self Esteem in the Classroom* Paul Chapman

Lipman, M., Sharp, A.M., and Oscanyan, F.S. (1980) *Philosophy in the Classroom* Philadelphia, Temple University Press

Nisbet, J. and Shucksmith, J., (1986) *Learning Strategies* Routledge and Kegan Paul

Reid, J., Forrestal, P., and Cook, J. (1982) *Small Group Work in the Classroom* Curriculum Branch Education Department of Western Australia.

Shayer, M. and Beasley, F. (1987) *Does Instrumental Enrichment Work?* British Educational Research Journal, Volume 13, No. 2

Sternberg, R.J. (1985) 'Approaches to Intelligence' in Chipman, S.F., Segal, J.W., and Glaser, R. (eds) *Thinking and Learning Skills: Research and Open Questions* (Vol 2). Hillsdale, New Jersey; Erlbaum

Stott, D.H. (1976) *Bristol Social Adjustment Guides Manual,* London, Hodder and Stoughton

Vernon, P.E. (1969) *Intelligence and Cultural Environment* London, Methuen

Vygotsky, L. (1978) *Mind in Society*: Cambridge, M.A., Harvard University Press

Weller, K. and Croft, A. (1983) *Making up our Minds: An Exploratory Study of Instrumental Enrichment.* Schools Council

Wiltshire Oracy Project, c/o Gilbert's Hill Infants School, Dixon Street, Swindon, Wiltshire SN1 3PL

Witkin, H.A. and Goodenough, D.R. (1977 December) *Field Dependence Revisited* (Research Bulletin 71-16). Princeton, New Jersey, Educational Testing Service.